MW00805653

the

Happy (Happy!!!) Holiday
Pot Cookie-Swap Cookbook

· Dr. Seymour Kindbud ·

13-Digit ISBN: 978-1604332384
10-Digit ISBN: 1604332387

This book may be ordered by mail from the publisher. Please include $2.50 for postage and handling.
Please support your local bookseller first!

Books published by Cider Mill Press Book Publishers are available at special discounts for bulk purchases in the United States by corporations, institutions, and other organizations. For more information, please contact the publisher.

Cider Mill Press Book Publishers
"Where good books are ready for press"
12 Port Farm Road
Kennebunkport, Maine 04046

Visit us on the Web!
www.cidermillpress.com

Design by Melissa Gerber
Typography: SignPainter, TodaySB
All illustrations and photography courtesy of Shutterstock.com.
Printed in China

1 2 3 4 5 6 7 8 9 0
First Edition

Contents

Cannabis meets Christmas. Can it get any better than this? You and all your friends gather for an evening of merriment, and everyone leaves with a cache of cookies to enjoy for the rest of the holiday season. But here's the best part: You're stoned the whole time because these "special" Christmas cookies are made with Christmas bud!

The custom of cookie swaps is now woven into the fabric of American holiday celebrations. But you and I know that you and your posse aren't exactly a Norman Rockwell painting. No problem. It's the cookies that count! You're just joining two traditions—getting stoned from sweets and swapping cookies at Christmas.

When Alice B. Toklas, the ganga Julia Child, started adding some hash to her brownies she probably never envisioned that there would be a whole book about chewing cheeba cookies to celebrate the holiday season. But that's what *The Happy (Happy!!!) Holiday Pot Cookie-Swap Cookbook* is all about. Right here in this volume is a whole game plan so you and your friends can light up like the proverbial Christmas tree without lighting up! You're ingesting all the goodness and savoring flavors as well as getting high.

Indeed you can get a good buzz on from ingesting weed. It's a longer-lasting high than you get from smoking it, but it takes longer to kick in than taking that first deep toke. Starting a little stoned makes the whole cooking process ever more enjoyable, too.

When making the easy treats in this book you'll find that within minutes you can be nibbling and noshing your way to a great high—deliciously. What carries the flavors in food is the fat, and when that fat has been infused with THC, the magical chemical that gives you the buzz from boom, Nirvana has been reached. Why roll a joint when you can get just as high from Sugar Weed Spritz (page 129) or Reefer Rolled-Out Sugar Cookies (page 48)?

The sneaky part about baking with weed is that you can get stoned anywhere at any time. At the movies? On a plane? While working? Sure. Your little home-baked hooch treats are your new BFF. Plus you can plan a whole party around cookies made with pot.

You may think that you're no Betty Crocker, and baking is hard. But you're wrong. I'm new to the world of cooking—cannabis and otherwise. And now I'm a kitchen geek. In fact I had so much fun writing my first cookbook—*Stoner Snacks*—that it just seemed natural to keep on truckin' with the holidays fast approaching. I was aided by being taught to cook and bake by this foxy woman who is better than any generic Betty Crocker. But I'll be your coach now. If I can make these cookies and candies, anyone can.

This holiday season, be part of the subculture of homes in which millions of cookies are swapped annually. But with your party the goods just keep on giving.

Happy baking!

Dr. Seymour Kindbud

CHAPTER 1:

· ·

The Strategy of Swaps

The idea of a party the purpose of which is to bring home a cache of cookies is more American than apple pie—which originated in England.

There's no Christopher Columbus or Thomas Edison identified as the Big Kahuna of cookie swaps, and no one claims to have given the first one. They seem to have become popular by the mid-twentieth century, and a reference to cookie swaps appears in a Betty Crocker cookbook in 1963.

Perhaps the swap that gets the longevity prize goes to a group of ladies in Wellesley,

Massachusetts. They started swapping sweets in 1971, and now there's a third generation of bakers in the wings. We don't know if these budding bakers will be baking with bud, but they could be.

The nice ladies of suburban Boston and their swap were made famous by Susan Mahnke Peery, the food editor of *Yankee* magazine, in 1986. She collected 200 of their recipes and added her own to *The Wellesley Cookie Exchange Cookbook*, and that popularized the custom from coast to coast, or from sea to shining sea.

There's the background. But I know you're holding this book because the idea of a whole party planned around exchanging treats with a twist appeals to you. And why not? Variety is the spice of life, and cookies can contain both spices and swag. A swap party is also a time to celebrate the season with friends who share your interests—eating sweets and getting stoned together while you do it.

In this chapter you'll learn the mechanics of a swap party, and I'll give you some tips to make your kitchen life easier during all seasons.

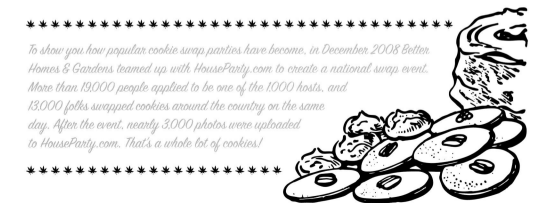

✳ ✳

To show you how popular cookie swap parties have become, in December 2008 Better Homes & Gardens teamed up with HouseParty.com to create a national swap event. More than 19,000 people applied to be one of the 1,000 hosts, and 13,000 folks swapped cookies around the country on the same day. After the event, nearly 3,000 photos were uploaded to HouseParty.com. That's a whole lot of cookies!

✳ ✳ ✳ ✳ ✳ ✳ ✳ ✳ ✳ ✳ ✳ ✳ ✳ ✳ ✳ ✳ ✳ ✳ ✳

More than a lot of other types of parties, a cookie swap requires lots of coordination by the host or hosts. It's not just getting a bunch of friends together. There's also making sure that everyone leaves with a selection of cookies, all of which are delicious, and all of which meet the party's first and most important criteria that they contain enough Bong Butter (page 23) and other augmented ingredients to get you high. So the first suggestion is to have everyone buy this book! If you're really generous you'll send it along with your invitation. This little tome is the Bible of bong hit sweets.

Here's a timetable and other steps to follow. Some people call them "rules" because they think the word implies authority. I, however, call them "guidelines" because your friends know you don't really have authority.

1. Compile your guest list of at least ten and not more than twenty fellow bakers. You want enough folks that everyone gets a variety of cookies, but there are only so many cookies that anyone wants, especially because these can't be fed to kids.

2. Insist that all cookies be homemade and good quality, so think about who in your circle are good cooks when making up the guest list. We know the cookies will have to be homemade until the government legalizes pot and a chain of cheeba bakeries goes national. But you don't want people showing up with a tray of burnt cookies that look like an offering to an extinct god.

3. Send your invitations a month in advance, and put a firm RSVP date of just ten days later. If folks aren't coming you'll still have time to fill in with others.

4. Give both a start and—perhaps more importantly—an end time for the cookie swap. You don't want to find guests around in anticipation of the Easter Bunny they've been there so long.

5. As part of the RSVP, ask everyone to send the name and description of what cookie they plan to bring. This list is key to a successful swap. Maybe in your house you called it Aunt Mary Jane's Bonker Brownies and in a friend's house it was called Kona Gold Brownies, but from the description they sound almost identical, so the guest who submitted it first gets to bake it.

6. Be vigilant about telling guests to pick again. The first-come, first-served rule is operative here. The first person that claims a cookie gets to bring it.

7. Decide how many cookies folks should bring by the guest count of the party. If it's an *intime* group of ten, then six dozen will do it. That's a half dozen for everyone to swap and a dozen to munch at the party. If the group is larger, up the number of cookies to seven or eight dozen.

8. Ask everyone to email you his or her recipe in advance. It's really nice to have a little booklet as a parting gift along with a selection of pot-laced treats.

9. Encourage guests to dress in their holiday finest. This is a time for the sweater your maiden aunt gave you with the reindeer on the front, or the earrings or tie that have blinking lights. A pot cookie swap is not the place for the LBD (that's Little Black Dress for those of you not up on fashion jargon) or the jeans with holes and work shirt.

10. Send a reminder email one week before the party to everyone who is coming. Remind them about the party itself. We all know how a bit of weed can make one a bit forgetful. And with your reminder, remind them to bring a container or cookie jar to transport their bounty of bong cookies home.

HOSTING WITHOUT HASSLES

Getting out the invites is the most important thing you've got to think about. No invites? No party. But there's still more to do.

The first step is envisioning where everything is going to go. You need a pretty table for the cookies that will get devoured in the course of the party, but then you also need an area where guests can deposit their cookies that will be swapped at the end of the evening. The idea of watching a dozen folks walk into your place with armloads of cookies is magical, but I never know where to put everyone's coat much less a caravan cum cookies.

Plan a menu in addition to sweets. You just can't munch cookies all evening. You've

got to think of savory nibbles, too. Cookies are the main event, but you don't want your friends to go into sugar shock. Plan on some dips and other nibbles. If you want to have some with a bit of buzz of their own, check out the recipes in my first cookbook, *Stoner Snacks*, for inspiration and ideas.

You also have to think about refreshments

of the liquid variety. Even cheeba cookies go great with milk, but they also go well with spiked eggnog. In fact, if you look at the method to make Booze with Buzz (page 26) the eggnog fits right in with the theme of the event.

Don't forget to decorate your place. It's a Christmas cookie swap party, not an evening to listen to the Grateful Dead! I bet that way down inside you there's a Martha Stewart microchip just waiting to be activated. Even if you have no holiday decorations elsewhere, tart up the room where the cookies are going to be. Wrap a few boxes to create different heights for the platters of cookies on the table. Cezanne did it in still life paintings, and good old Paulie doesn't mind if you borrow his idea.

Remember that our noses are part of the whole sensory experience, too. Burn scented candles for atmosphere, or boil some cinnamon sticks and cloves on the stove to add fragrance to the fête.

Bring in aural excitement too. Don't think you have to bore friends with the Mormon Tabernacle Choir. Go to iTunes and download a bunch of hip holiday tunes to play in the background. And don't forget such contemporary classics as "Grandma Got Run Over by a Reindeer."

Because cannabis didn't play a big role in Judeo-Christian religion or the cultures that spawned it, it doesn't come as a shock that it wasn't appreciated much in the New World. It was likely brought to South America by the Spanish conquistadors, and in colonial America hemp was second only to cotton in importance as a crop. It was introduced to Jamestown, Virginia, in 1611 and Plymouth, Massachusetts, in 1632. But it was totally wasted by those uptight Puritans, who used it just to make cloth and rope.

ENVISIONING THE EVENT

A party is really like a piece of performance art. You've got the set (your house or apartment) and the actors (aka guests). But what you need to do is come up with a good plot line, or in this case, think through how to keep the party going and make sure everyone is having a good time. If you plan in advance you'll find that the party really goes on cruise control and you end up having as good a time as your guests.

If your guests don't know each other, break the ice with some party games and gather some really dorky prizes for them. You could promise a gift to the first person who sends in an RSVP. It's one way to get people to respond.

You can have lots of loony contests, and have everyone vote by secret ballot with prizes awarded at the end. It doesn't have to be all sugary; after all, the reason for this party is pot cookies!

Here are some possible categories:

- Cookie you wish you had made instead of the one you did.
- Cookie that should be banned from future swaps.
- Holiday outfit that everyone wants to wear next year.
- Holiday outfit that should be burned after the party.
- Best cookie name.
- Worst cookie description.

You can also do real games toward the end of the evening when the mood is mellow and everyone is stoned. Some variation of Pin the Tail on the Donkey, such as Pin the Joint on the Reindeer or Pin the Unmentionable Anatomical Part on the Gingerbread Man, is always popular. If you're feeling verbally creative try coming up with new and hip names for Santa's reindeer (surely something has to beat out Prancer and Dancer!) or come up with new verses for the "Twelve Days of Christmas."

And remember to take pictures of it all! You never know when times will be tough and having the fodder for blackmail might come in handy.

It's all been great. You and your buds nibbled bud and had a great time. But it's nearing the end time you put on the invitation. Now there's another logistical challenge: dividing up the cookies.

This can lead to bedlam if not handled with a plan in mind. The way I've done it with the least chaos is to first clear the table of the cookies you've been munching during the party. Once you've got an open area, tell everyone to place their take-away containers on the table.

The last part of it is then pretty easy. A few folks at a time grab their cache of swapping cookies and dole them out. Soon the once-empty containers on the table are filled with the same array of treats you've been enjoying all evening. This is a signal that the party is over, and it's time for everyone to go home!

Devising a Cookie "Game Plan" for Your Own Baking

While you're baking for your cookie swap, kitchen efficiency becomes even more important because there's so much cooking to do, in addition to all the other activities that surround the approach of Christmas. If you only have a few hours to spend in the kitchen, you want to make sure your cookie production is high.

Start by making a pan of bar cookies; they are quick to assemble but they take the longest time to bake. Once they are in the oven, it's time to make the doughs for rolled cookies that need chilling before they can be baked.

The third type of cookie to make is a batch of drop cookies. The bars are out of the oven, and these cookies don't need chilling time, so they can bake while you roll and cut out the chilled doughs.

Almost all cookies in this book are baked at 350°F, so there's no need for the oven to ever be empty. If you choose a recipe that is baked at 375°F, make those after the other batches.

Cookie doughs are not only easy to make, they're just about indestructible. You can successfully freeze cookie dough and bake off individual cookies or a whole batch at a moment's notice, like when your friends are walking in the door and you decide that a cannabis creation is in order.

If you want to freeze a whole batch of dough, do so in a heavy resealable plastic bag, and allow it to thaw overnight in the refrigerator. But I find it's much easier to freeze individual dough balls.

Cover a baking sheet with plastic wrap, and form the proper size balls of dough on the cookie sheet. You can place them very close together because they're not going to spread. Once they are frozen solid, transfer them to a heavy resealable plastic bag. It's not necessary to allow time for frozen dough balls to thaw. Just add 2 to 3 minutes to the baking time of the cookie.

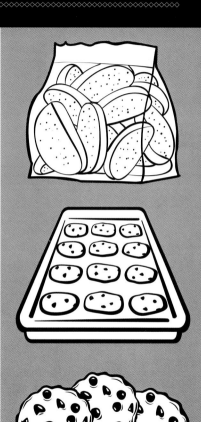

CHAPTER 2:

Becoming a Smart Cookie: How to Chew Your Cheeba and Baking Basics

Most of the ingredients you'll be using are the same boring ones that just get you fat, but now they'll get you fat *and* high. That's a big difference. You'll see sugar and spice, and everything nice too. But the key to marvelous moocha cookies is butter that's been infused with Christmas bud. Every cookie and candy recipe has it, and it's the wonder drug of weed. There are a few other ways to add more joy stick joy to your cookies, and those are listed in this chapter too.

As we discussed in Chapter 1, part of the cookie swap party is making cookies visually pop with decorations. At the end of this chapter are some glazes and tips for cookie decorating. Whether you admire Michelangelo or Modigliani, we know there's an artist inside you just bursting for a chance to show off.

☘ A Different Highway to High

What everyone finds during first forays of baking with cannabis is that the high is definitely there, but it's different from the high you get when you're puffing. Here's why that happens.

The ingredient that gets you high on pot is Tetrahydrocannabinol, or delta 9 THC for short. Although all parts of the plant contain this wonder substance, the buds have the highest level. The forms in which delta 9 THC are found in cannabis are many; they're called isomers, and at least fifty have been isolated of which only six are psychoactive. Some lead to euphoria, while others lead to relaxation, and some lead to drowsiness.

When you smoke weed and inhale deeply, the THC transfuses into your blood almost instantly thorough the thousands of capillaries located on the surface of the lungs. This reaction increases with how much time the smoke

is in contact with the capillaries, which is why inhaled smoke should be held in for as long as possible without turning blue.

From these capillaries, the THC enters the bloodstream. It then makes a beeline right to the brain and links up with receptors waiting for it like horny sailors hitting port. This transmission from the lungs to the brain is almost instantaneous, which is why you get high so quickly. But it wears off once the THC molecules no longer bind to the receptors.

Eating weed is a more complex physiological trip. When eaten, the THC is turned into a THC metabolite in the liver, and becomes a compound called 11-hydroxy-THC. The high from this THC derivative is actually more powerful than the lungs-to-brain high. But it starts slower. That's the bummer. It also can last for up to five hours. That's the plus, and which is why cooking with cannabis brings a sense of gourmet enjoyment, both through the food in which its cooked and the total experience of savoring.

You know how oil and water don't mix? Well, neither does THC and water. The only way to get the chemical into your food is via fat. That's why you have to infuse either butter or oil with weed to get the effects.

Another fact of cooking fu is that you get the best results once the weed is heated.

 ## Bong Butter

Bong Butter is the Mother's Milk of cannabis cookies and candies. The THC in the weed is transferred to the fat in the butter, and the water in which it's all boiling together keeps it from scorching.

Making Bong Butter is more a method and formula than a recipe, and you can do a few pounds of butter at a time; it keeps for a few weeks refrigerated or frozen for up to six months. But it never lasts that long in my house! And it certainly won't last that long when making these cookies either.

The formulation is 1 stick of unsalted butter (¼ pound) per ¼ to ½ ounce of weed. This recipe is for up to 1 pound of Bong Butter. Adding more water to the pan can scale it up.

Bring a few cups of water to a boil in a saucepan, and while the water is heating, grind up your weed in a special grinder reserved for this purpose, or in a mortar

and pestle. Melt your butter in the boiling water, and stir in the ground weed. Reduce the heat to low, and cover the pan. Simmer for 2 hours, stirring it occasionally.

Strain the liquid into a bowl through a fine-mesh sieve lined with a few layers of cheesecloth or a few paper coffee filters. Let the liquid sit at room temperature until cool, and then cover it with plastic wrap and refrigerate it overnight, or until the butter on top of the liquid has formed a solid layer. There's no magic about overnight, but it does take up to eight hours, depending on how much you made.

Just pull off the solid stuff and throw out the liquid stuff. *Voilà!* You've got a stash of Bong Butter.

Bhang Booster

While in India *bhang* is a drink unto itself, this variation—made with evaporated milk so that it has a long life refrigerated—is used as an ingredient in many recipes. Because it's heated during the infusing cycle, it can be used cold in dishes and deliver its desired buzz. There's enough fat in regular evaporated milk for all the THC goodies find a good home, so don't buy any low-fat versions.

Combine 1 (12-ounce) can of evaporated milk with ½ ounce of pulverized weed in a small saucepan. Bring it to a simmer over medium heat, stirring it occasionally. Reduce the heat to low, and simmer for 10 minutes. Strain it through a paper coffee filter. Press hard to get as much liquid out of the weed as possible. Then store it refrigerated.

Booze with Buzz

In addition to being soluble in oil, THC also does well in booze, which can be used in baking, too, or just poured over some ice cubes. The formulation for Booze with Buzz is ¼ ounce of weed per 3 ounces of liquor.

Pound the weed into a powder with a mortar and pestle, and soak it overnight in water. This gets rid of any dirt on the weed but doesn't take away from the THC. Then drain it off and pour booze over it in a little jar. Hide the jar in a cool dark place (like alongside your vanilla extract), and let it mellow for 2 weeks, shaking it every day.

Strain it through a paper coffee filter. Press hard to get as much liquid out of the weed as possible. Then store it refrigerated. Like all pot-potent foods, this has to be heated to activate its goodies, but you'll find lots of ways to do that later in this book.

Baking Basics

Baking cookies is not rocket science, which is perhaps why it's the first kitchen activity most of us undertook as children. While cooking is a form of art, when it comes to baking, science class enters the equation as well. Savory recipes may be tolerant of virtually endless substitutions, but baked goods like cookies are not. Each ingredient performs a specific function in a recipe based on a certain quantity to create a batter or dough.

These are general pointers on procedures to be used for all genres of baked goods:

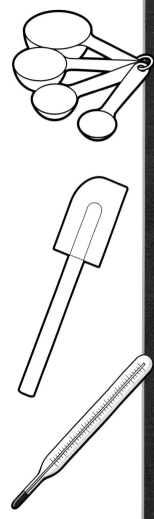

- **Measure accurately.** Measure dry ingredients in dry measuring cups, which are plastic or metal, and come in sizes of ¼, ⅓, ½, and 1 cup. Spoon dry ingredients from the container or canister into the measuring cup, and then sweep the top with a straight edge such as the back of a knife or a spatula to measure it properly. Do not dip the cup into the canister or tap it on the counter to produce a level surface. These methods pack down the dry ingredients, and can increase the actual volume by up to 10 percent. Tablespoons and teaspoons should also be leveled; a rounded ½ teaspoon can really measure almost 1 teaspoon. If the box or can does not have a straight edge built in, level the excess in the spoon back into the container with the back of a knife blade. Measure liquids in liquid measures, which come in different sizes but are transparent glass or plastic and have lines on the sides. To accurately measure liquids, place the measuring cup on a flat counter, then bend down to read the marked level.

- **Create consistent temperature.** All ingredients should be at room temperature unless otherwise indicated. Having all ingredients at the same temperature makes it easier to combine them into a smooth, homogeneous mixture. Adding cold liquid to a dough or batter can cause the batter to lose its unified structure by making the fat rigid.

- **Preheat the oven.** Some ovens can take up to 25 minutes to reach a high temperature, such as 450°F. The minimum heating time should be 15 minutes.

- **Plan ahead.** Read the recipe thoroughly, and assemble all your ingredients. This means that you have accounted for all ingredients required for a recipe in advance, so you don't get to a step and realize you must improvise. Assembling in advance also lessens the risk of over-mixing dough or batters, as the mixer drones on while you search for a specific spice or bag of chips.

 ## Careful Creaming

Perhaps the most vital step in the creation of cookie dough is the "creaming" of the butter and sugar. During this process, air is beaten in and is trapped in the butter's crystalline structure. It is the number and size of the air bubbles (which then become enlarged by the carbon dioxide produced by baking soda or baking powder) that leavens a dough or batter to produce a high, finely textured product.

The starting point in proper creaming is to ensure that the

butter is at the correct temperature, approximately 70°F. Remove the Bong Butter from the refrigerator and cut it or scoop it into small pieces, like about the size of a large marble. Allow them to sit at room temperature for 15 to 20 minutes to soften.

Begin creaming by beating the butter alone in a mixer until it has broken into small pieces. Then add the sugar, and beat at medium speed to start the process of combining them. Then increase the speed to high, and scrape the bowl frequently. When properly creamed, the texture of the butter and sugar mixture will be light and fluffy.

Chocolate 101

The key to the success for all chocolate cookies and candies is to use a high-quality product. The old saying of "garbage in, garbage out" applies here, too.

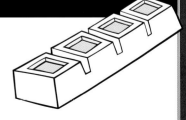

It's also important (with the following exceptions) to use the type of chocolate specified in the recipe because the amount of additional sugar and other ingredients are calculated according to the sweetness level of the chocolate. If you use a different chocolate, things could taste off.

Here's a quick guide to chocolate:

- **Unsweetened.** Also referred to as baking or bitter chocolate, this is the purest of all cooking chocolate. It is hardened chocolate liquor (the essence of the cocoa bean, not an alcohol) that contains no sugar. It is usually packaged in a bar of eight (1-ounce) blocks. According to the U.S. standard of identity, unsweetened chocolate must contain 50 to 58 percent cocoa butter.

- **Bittersweet.** This chocolate is slightly sweetened with sugar; the amount varies depending on the manufacturer. This chocolate must contain 35 percent chocolate liquor and should be used when intense chocolate flavor is desired. Also use it interchangeably with semisweet chocolate in cooking and baking.

- **Semisweet.** This chocolate is sweetened with sugar, but unlike bittersweet it also can have added flavorings such as vanilla. It is available in bar form as well as chips and pieces.

- **Sweet cooking.** This chocolate must contain 15 percent chocolate liquor, and it almost always has a higher sugar content than semisweet chocolate. It is usually found in 4-ounce bars.

- **Milk.** This is a mild-flavored chocolate used primarily for candy bars but rarely (except for milk chocolate chips) in cooking. It can have as little as 10 percent chocolate liquor but must contain 12 percent milk solids.

- **Unsweetened cocoa powder.** This is powdered chocolate that has had a portion of the cocoa butter removed. Cocoa keeps indefinitely in a cool place.
- **Dutch process cocoa powder.** This type of cocoa powder is formulated with reduced acidity and gives foods a more mellow flavor. However, it also burns at a lower temperature than more common cocoa.

SUBBING WITH SUCCESS

Bittersweet, semisweet, and sweet chocolate can be used interchangeably in recipes, depending on personal taste. Most chocolate desserts tend to be sweet, so it's better to go from a semisweet to a bittersweet rather than the other direction.

Do not substitute chocolate chips and bits of broken chocolate for one another. Chocolate chips are formulated to retain their shape at high heat and react differently when baked than chopped chocolate does. Chocolate chips can form gritty granules in a cooled dessert.

HANDLE WITH CARE

Except when you're eating chocolate out of your hand or folding chips into cookie dough, chocolate needs a bit of special handling. Use these tips when dealing with the common tasks associated with chocolate:

Chopping chocolate. Chopping chocolate into fine pieces makes melting easier. You can do this in a food processor fitted with a steel blade. Begin by breaking it with a heavy knife rather than breaking it with your hands. Body heat is sufficiently high enough to soften the chocolate so it will not chop evenly.

Melting chocolate. Most chocolate needs careful melting because it scorches easily. You can melt it in a number of ways:

- Melt chunks in the top of a double boiler placed over barely simmering water.

- Melt chopped chocolate in a microwave-safe bowl, and microwave on Medium (50 percent power) for 30 seconds. Stir, and repeat as necessary.

- Preheat the oven to 250°F. Place the chopped chocolate in the oven and then turn off the heat immediately. Stir after 3 minutes, and return to the warm oven if necessary.

With all these methods, melt the chocolate until it is just about smooth; the heat in the chocolate will complete the process.

An easy way to dress up bar cookies is by drizzling the pan with dark chocolate or white chocolate before cutting the cookies into pieces. Once the chocolate is melted, dip a spoon into it and then wave the spoon over the cookie pan. An alternate method is to place the melted chocolate in a heavy resealable plastic bag, and cut off the tip of one corner.

Becoming a Pastry Picasso

Chagall made stained glass windows, and you're going to make Stained Glass Cookies! Part of the high at a cookie swap comes from having all your buddies tell you that your bud creations are just gorgeous—as well as delicious. And it's really not hard to do.

CONFECTIONERS' SUGAR GLAZE

This is the easiest and most basic way to cover cooled cookies, and it hardens really hard in less than an hour.

YIELD: 1½ cups
ACTIVE TIME: 5 minutes
START TO FINISH: 5 minutes

4 cups (1 pound) confectioners' sugar
4 to 5 tablespoons water
½ teaspoon clear vanilla extract
Food coloring (optional)

Combine confectioners' sugar, 4 tablespoons water, and vanilla in a mixing bowl. Stir until smooth, adding additional water if too thick.

If tinting glaze, transfer it to small cups and add food coloring, a few drops at a time, until desired color is reached. Stir well before adding additional coloring.

NOTE: The glaze can be kept at room temperature in an airtight container, with a sheet of plastic wrap pressed directly into the surface, for up 6 hours. Beat it again lightly to emulsify before using.

VARIATIONS:

• Substitute orange juice concentrate for the water and orange extract for the vanilla. Make this variation only if you plan to color the glaze because it won't be white.

• Substitute peppermint oil or almond extract for the vanilla.

HOW TO USE:

This glaze is not strong enough to hold large candies, but it can be used as "glue" for small items like jimmies. One way to use it is to spread the white glaze on cooled cookies and allow it to dry hard. Then mix 1 teaspoon of water into ¼ cup of the glaze, and tint it with food coloring. Crumple up a sheet of waxed paper and dip it into the tinted glaze; then dab the cookies and you'll have a marbled effect.

ROYAL ICING

This is the formulation for the shiny icing used on cookies once they're baked and cooled. This frosting can only be used on cookies kept at room temperature because refrigerating the cookies can cause the frosting to become sticky.

YIELD: 3½ cups
ACTIVE TIME: 5 minutes
START TO FINISH: 12 minutes

3 large egg whites, at room temperature
½ teaspoon cream of tartar
¼ teaspoon salt
4 cups (1 pound) confectioners' sugar
½ teaspoon pure vanilla extract
Food coloring (optional)

1. Place egg whites in a grease-free mixing bowl and beat at medium speed with an electric mixer until frothy. Add the cream of tartar and salt, raise the speed to high, and beat until soft peaks form.

2. Add sugar and beat at low speed to moisten. Raise the speed to high, and beat for 5 to 7 minutes, or until mixture is glossy and stiff peaks form. Beat in vanilla.

3. If tinting icing, transfer it to small cups and add food coloring, a few drops at a time, until desired color is reached. Stir well before adding additional coloring.

NOTE: The icing can be kept at room temperature in an airtight container for up to 2 days. Beat it again lightly to emulsify before using.

VARIATION:

• Substitute peppermint oil, almond extract, lemon oil, or orange oil for the vanilla.

HOW TO USE:

Royal Icing of this consistency is perfect to pipe decorations onto cooled cookies, and you can also use it as the "glue" to affix big candies. If you want to paint the cookies with frosting, thin the icing with milk 1 teaspoon at a time until the proper consistency is reached.

BONGED UP BUTTERCREAM ICING

This icing is richer than Royal Icing and delivers its own wacky weed quotient to a cookie. It's not truly white because of the butter, and it does harden somewhat but not into a true glaze. Use it to fill sandwich cookies or as a frosting for cupcakes and cakes.

YIELD: 2½ cups
ACTIVE TIME: 5 minutes
START TO FINISH: 5 minutes

½ cup Bong Butter (page 23), softened
4 cups (1 pound) confectioners' sugar
3 tablespoons whole milk
1 teaspoon pure vanilla extract
Food coloring (optional)

1. Place butter, sugar, milk, and vanilla in a large mixing bowl. Beat at low speed with an electric mixer to blend. Increase the speed to high, and beat for 2 minutes, or until light and fluffy.

2. If tinting icing, transfer it to small cups and add food coloring, a few drops at a time, until desired consistency is reached. Stir well before adding additional coloring.

NOTE: The icing can be kept refrigerated in an airtight container for up to 5 days. Bring it to room temperature before using.

VARIATIONS:
• Substitute almond extract, lemon oil, or orange oil for the vanilla.

HOW TO USE:
Buttercream is a wonderful icing to use to make rosettes or other complex decorations with a pastry bag. If not stiff enough, add additional confectioners' sugar 1 tablespoon at a time.

EGG PAINT

Mixing beaten egg yolks with food coloring produces far more vibrant colors than can be created with Royal Icing. It's like the tempera paint used in Medieval European churches.

Whisk about 4 or 5 egg yolks well, and divide them into different small cups. Add food coloring at about the ratio of $\frac{1}{2}$ teaspoon per egg yolk, or more if you want really bright colors, and stir well.

Start by drawing a design on the cookies with the tip of a paring knife; the grooves will keep the colors from running into each other. Then use a small paintbrush to apply the color to cookies before they are baked. The colors will darken slightly in the oven and the cookies will also have an attractive shiny glaze.

USING CANDIES AND CONFECTIONS

The collection of colored and flavored sweets that can be affixed to cookies is almost endless. Some of them should be applied before the cookies are baked, and others need to be "glued" on with Royal Icing once the cookies have cooled.

As a general rule, any candy that can melt, like hard candies, miniature marshmallows, or jellybeans, should be applied after cooking, and any candy that is basically an ingredient, such as the coarse colored sugars found around the holidays, gold or silver dragées, nuts, or candied fruit, should be used before baking. Ingredients like raisins can be used either way. If they are the "eyes" of gingerbread people or snowmen, place them before baking, but if they're ornaments on a wreath, add them after the cookie has been frosted.

A way to use colored sugars after cookies are baked is to create patterns with stencils. Spread either Royal Icing or Confectioners' Sugar Glaze on the cooled cookie, and then place a stencil made from parchment paper over it. Sprinkle sugars or jimmies through the hole in the stencil.

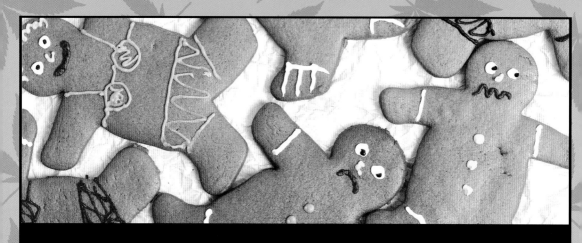

CHAPTER 3:

. . . .

DTD (Decorated to Death): Rolled and Formed Cookies

When you think "Christmas Cookie" it's the recipes in this chapter that pop into your mind like visions of sugarplums, whatever they are. They sound great, but who knows what they actually taste like.

Here are those flat things topped with colored icing and candies. Also in this group are gingerbread people, which, if you're really artistic, you can make anatomically correct, either before or after baking.

Here's a trick I learned from a professional baker that makes keeping the cookies looking good easier. Once the dough is rolled and you've used a cutter to create your shape, it's easier to remove the excess dough rather than trying to move the delicate cookies to the baking sheets. This process is similar to what artists term "relief sculpture." What you are doing is pulling out what is not needed to leave what you want. If you rolled and cut the cookies on a sheet of waxed paper, all you have to do is invert it onto the cookie sheet.

✦ An Alternative Approach

Rolling dough takes some manual dexterity and coordination. Sometimes you really dig doing it when you're stoned, and at other times the dough looks like a rutted road in the spring. Fear not, help from Dr. Kindbud is here. If you can cut a sheet of waxed paper, you can make good-looking cookies.

Most of these recipes can also be baked from chilled logs of dough. There's a whole category called "refrigerator cookies" that fit this bill. You form the dough into a log, and you make the log even by rolling it gently on the counter in the waxed paper. Then you refrigerate the log until it's really firm. Rather than any sort of laborious rolling, you cut off slices from the log and bake them. Some cookies are even written for this method, but most can be adapted to it.

If you want to make them pretty, decorate them with colored sugar or candies before you bake them, or decorate them with icing after they're cooled.

You can actually hang refrigerator cookies on a small tree as edible ornaments for your cookie swap party. Before baking them, create a small hole at the top with the tip of a paring knife, and make sure the holes have not closed up when the cookies come out of the oven. Loop ribbon through the hole after the cookies cool.

BONKER BOYS GINGERBREAD COOKIES

Hey, you can do gingerbread girls as well as gingerbread boys, and if you want to get creative with any bits of dough you have left you can make them "anatomically correct." These have lots of flavor from lots of spices.

YIELD: 3 dozen (3-inch) cookies
ACTIVE TIME: 25 minutes
START TO FINISH: 1¾ hours, including 1 hour to chill dough

¾ cup (12 tablespoons) Bong Butter (page 23), softened
½ cup firmly packed light brown sugar
⅔ cup unsulfured molasses
1 large egg, at room temperature
1 teaspoon baking soda
1 teaspoon ground ginger
1 teaspoon apple pie spice
½ teaspoon salt
½ teaspoon pure vanilla extract
¼ teaspoon freshly ground black pepper
3 cups all-purpose flour
Royal Icing (page 36) or Confectioners' Sugar Glaze (page 34)
Small candies (optional)

1. Combine butter and sugar in a mixing bowl, and beat at low speed with an electric mixer to blend. Increase the speed to high, and beat for 3 to 4 minutes, or until light and fluffy. Beat in molasses, egg, baking soda, ginger, apple pie spice, salt, vanilla, and pepper, and beat for 1 minute. Slowly add flour to butter mixture, and beat until stiff dough forms.

2. Divide dough in half, and wrap each half in plastic wrap. Press dough into a pancake. Refrigerate dough for 1 hour or until firm or up to 2 days.

3. Preheat the oven to 350°F. Line two baking sheets with parchment paper or silicon baking mats.

4. Lightly dust a sheet of waxed paper and a rolling pin with flour. Roll dough to a thickness of ⅛ inch. Dip cookie cutters in flour, and cut out cookies. Remove excess dough, and transfer cookies to the baking sheets. Re-roll excess dough, chilling it for 15 minutes if necessary.

5. Bake cookies for 10 to 12 minutes, or until firm. Cool cookies for 2 minutes on the baking sheets, and then transfer cookies to racks to cool completely. Decorate cooled cookies with Royal Icing or Confectioners' Sugar Glaze, and candies, if using.

NOTE: Keep cookies in an airtight container, layered between sheets of waxed paper or parchment, at room temperature for up to 5 days. Cookies can also be frozen for up to 2 months. Do not freeze cookies if decorated.

VARIATION:

- Add ½ cup chopped raisins to the dough, and bake the cookies as drop cookies for 13 to 15 minutes. No chilling is necessary for a drop cookie.

Apple pie spice is a combination of fragrant spices that are pre-blended, so you don't have to purchase all of them individually. You can make your own by combining ½ teaspoon cinnamon, ¼ teaspoon nutmeg, ⅛ teaspoon allspice, ⅛ teaspoon ground cardamom, and ¼ teaspoon ground cloves. Or, in a pinch, substitute cinnamon as the primary base, with a dash of any of the other spices you might have on hand.

✳ ✳

REEFER ROLLED-OUT SUGAR COOKIES

Fancy shapes and pretty colors are what Christmas sugar cookies are all about, and these also deliver dynamite flavor as well as a good buzz. I sometimes make some batches and freeze them early in the fall and then decorate them closer to the holidays.

YIELD: 2 to 3 dozen, depending on the size of the cutters
ACTIVE TIME: 30 minutes
START TO FINISH: 1¾ hours, including 1 hour to chill dough

¾ cup (12 tablespoons) Bong Butter (page 23), softened
¾ cup granulated sugar
1 large egg, at room temperature
1 teaspoon pure vanilla extract
½ teaspoon salt
2½ cups all-purpose flour
Royal Icing (page 36), optional
Confectioners' Sugar Glaze (page 34), optional
Assorted small candies, optional

1. Combine butter and sugar in a mixing bowl, and beat at low speed with an electric mixer to blend. Increase the speed to high, and beat for 3 to 4 minutes, or until light and fluffy. Beat in egg, vanilla, and salt, and beat for 1 minute. Slowly add flour to butter mixture, and beat until stiff dough forms.

2. Divide dough in half, and wrap each half in plastic wrap. Press dough into a pancake. Refrigerate dough for 1 hour or until firm, or up to 2 days.

3. Preheat the oven to 350°F. Line two baking sheets with parchment paper or silicon baking mats.

4. Lightly dust a sheet of waxed paper and a rolling pin with flour. Roll dough to a thickness of ¼ inch. Dip cookie cutters in flour, and cut out cookies. Remove excess dough, and transfer cookies to the baking sheets. Re-roll excess dough, chilling it for 15 minutes if necessary.

5. Bake cookies for 10 to 12 minutes, or until edges are brown. Cool cookies for 2 minutes on the baking sheets, and then transfer cookies to racks to cool completely. Decorate cooled cookies with Royal Icing, Confectioners' Sugar Glaze, and candies, if desired.

NOTE: Keep cookies in an airtight container, layered between sheets of waxed paper or parchment, at room temperature for up to 5 days. Cookies can also be frozen for up to 2 months. Do not freeze cookies if decorated.

VARIATIONS:

- Substitute lemon oil for the vanilla extract, and add 2 teaspoon grated lemon zest to the dough.

- Beat the egg with ¼ teaspoon food coloring before adding it to the dough.

- Add 1½ teaspoons ground cardamom and 1 tablespoon grated orange zest to the dough.

✶✶

Don't have a rolling pin? Or your rolling pin is keeping your window propped open? No problem. Cover a glass wine bottle or any sort of round bottle with aluminum foil. Voilà! You've got a rolling pin!

✶✶

PSYCHEDELIC STAINED GLASS COOKIES

These are basically sugar cookies with a subtle rum flavor, but what makes them cool is that you bake them with crushed hard candy in holes cut out from the dough so that they look like stained glass windows when they're cooked.

YIELD: 3 to 4 dozen, depending on the size of the cutters
ACTIVE TIME: 30 minutes
START TO FINISH: 2 hours, including 1 hour to chill dough

1 cup (16 tablespoons) Bong Butter (page 23), softened
¾ cup granulated sugar
½ cup firmly packed light brown sugar
1 large egg, at room temperature
½ teaspoon rum extract
½ teaspoon salt
3¼ cups all-purpose flour
1 (7-ounce) package brightly colored hard candy, such as sour balls

1. Combine butter, granulated sugar, and brown sugar in a mixing bowl, and beat at low speed with an electric mixer to combine. Increase the speed to high, and beat for 3 to 4 minutes, or until light and fluffy. Beat in egg, rum extract, and salt, and beat for 1 minute. Slowly add flour to butter mixture, and beat until stiff dough forms.

2. Divide dough in half, and wrap each half in plastic wrap. Press dough into a pancake. Refrigerate dough for 1 hour or until firm, or up to 2 days.

3. While dough chills, divide the candies into groupings by color in separate heavy-duty plastic bags. Pound candies with the bottom of a small saucepan until crushed.

4. Preheat the oven to 350°F. Line two baking sheets with parchment paper or silicon baking mats.

5. Lightly dust a sheet of waxed paper and a rolling pin with flour. Roll dough to a thickness of ¼ inch. Dip cookie cutters in flour, and cut out cookies. Remove excess dough, and transfer cookies to the baking sheets. Use smaller cutters to create designs inside of larger cookies. Re-roll excess dough, chilling it for 15 minutes if necessary. Fill holes in cookies with crushed candy.

6. Bake cookies for 10 to 12 minutes, or until edges are brown. Cool cookies for 2 minutes on the baking sheets, and then transfer cookies to racks to cool completely.

NOTE: Keep cookies in an airtight container, layered between sheets of waxed paper or parchment, at room temperature for up to 5 days.

VARIATION:

- Substitute orange oil for the rum extract, and add 1 tablespoon grated orange zest to the dough.

If you don't have enough cooling racks for cookies, start them on the rack and then transfer them to sheets of plastic wrap onto which granulated sugar has been sprinkled. The sugar will keep the bottoms from sticking.

WHACKY WEED CORNMEAL COOKIES

Cornmeal gives these cookies some extra texture than just crispy. But they're still light in color, so paint them before baking them for some visual zing too.

YIELD: 2 to 3 dozen
ACTIVE TIME: 20 minutes
START TO FINISH: 2¾ hours, including 2 hours to chill dough

½ cup (8 tablespoons) Bong Butter (page 23), softened
¾ cup confectioners' sugar
1 large egg, at room temperature
½ teaspoon pure vanilla extract
⅔ cup all-purpose flour
¼ cup finely ground yellow cornmeal
2 tablespoons cornstarch
¼ teaspoon salt
Colored sugars

1. Combine butter and sugar in a mixing bowl, and beat at low speed with an electric mixer to blend. Increase the speed to high, and beat for 3 to 4 minutes, or until light and fluffy. Beat in egg and vanilla, and beat for 1 minute. Slowly add flour, cornmeal, cornstarch, and salt to butter mixture, and beat until stiff dough forms.

2. Place dough on a sheet of waxed paper, and form it into a log 2½ inches in diameter. Refrigerate dough covered in plastic wrap for 2 hours, or until firm, or up to 2 days.

3. Preheat the oven to 350°F. Line two baking sheets with parchment paper or silicon baking mats.

4. Cut chilled dough into ⅓-inch slices using a sharp serrated knife, and arrange them on the baking sheets. Decorate cookies with sugar crystals.

5. Bake cookies for 10 to 12 minutes, or until edges are brown. Cool cookies for 2 minutes on the baking sheets, and then transfer cookies to racks to cool completely.

NOTE: Keep cookies in an airtight container, layered between sheets of waxed paper or parchment, at room temperature for up to 5 days. Cookies can also be frozen for up to 2 months. Do not freeze cookies if decorated.

VARIATION:

• Add ¾ cup chopped candied fruit to the dough, and bake them as a drop cookie.

Maybe the late William F. Buckley Jr. was conservative when it came to politics, but not to pot. He wrote: "Even if one takes every reefer madness allegation of the prohibitionists at face value, marijuana prohibition has done far more harm to far more people than marijuana ever could."

GINGERED GANGA SHORTBREAD SLIVERS

Shortbread is a classic English cookie that is full of buttery flavor, and in this case the crisp cookies are enlivened with some ganga in the butter as well as crystallized ginger to augment the flavor. Sprinkling them with colored sugar dresses them up.

YIELD: 2 dozen
ACTIVE TIME: 15 minutes
START TO FINISH: 45 minutes

1 cup (16 tablespoons) Bong Butter (page 23), softened
1½ cups granulated sugar
1 teaspoon pure vanilla extract
2 cups all-purpose flour
⅓ cup cornstarch
½ cup finely chopped crystallized ginger
Colored sugar crystals

1. Preheat the oven to 350°F, and grease two (10-inch) pie plates.

2. Combine butter, sugar, and vanilla in a mixing bowl, and beat at medium speed with an electric mixer until blended. Increase the speed to high, and beat until light and fluffy. Reduce the speed to low, and add flour, cornstarch, and ginger.

3. Press dough into the prepared pie plate, extending the sides up ½ inch. Cut dough into 12 thin wedges. Prick surface of dough all over with the tines of a fork. Pat dough with sugar crystals.

4. Bake for 30 minutes, or until dough is lightly browned at the edges. Remove the pans from the oven, and go over cut lines again. Cool completely in the pans on a wire rack, and then remove slivers from the pie plate with a small spatula.

NOTE: Keep cookies in an airtight container, layered between sheets of waxed paper or parchment, at room temperature for up to 5 days. Cookies can also be frozen for up to 2 months.

VARIATIONS:

• Substitute 1 cup miniature chocolate chips for the ginger.

• Substitute 1 cup slivered almonds, toasted in a 350°F oven for 5 to 7 minutes, or until lightly browned, for the ginger, and substitute pure almond extract for the vanilla extract.

• Substitute ½ cup dried cranberries for the ginger, and add 1 tablespoon grated orange zest to the dough.

- Add 1 teaspoon apple pie spice and beat it along with the butter and sugar, and substitute ½ cup raisins for the ginger.

✳ ✳

Crystallized ginger is fresh ginger that is preserved by being candied in sugar syrup. It's then tossed with coarse sugar. It's very expensive in little bottles in the spice aisle, but most whole foods markets sell it in bulk.

✳ ✳

❋ LOCO WEED LEMON COCONUT SANDWICH COOKIES

Move over Oreo! Now these are a tropical sandwich cookie that an adult can really appreciate. And with some bumped up butter in both the cookie and filling, you'll remember these taste treats for a long time.

YIELD: 4 dozen
ACTIVE TIME: 25 minutes
START TO FINISH: 3 hours, including 2 hours to chill dough

Cookies

1 cup sweetened shredded coconut

1 cup (16 tablespoons) Bong Butter (page 23), softened

⅓ cup granulated sugar

1 tablespoon grated lemon zest

1 teaspoon lemon oil

2 cups all-purpose flour

½ teaspoon salt

Colored sugar crystals (optional)

Filling

1 cup confectioners' sugar

¼ cup (4 tablespoons) Bong Butter (page 23), softened

1 tablespoon grated lemon zest

1 tablespoon freshly squeezed lemon juice

2 tablespoons light corn syrup

1. Preheat the oven to 325°F. Place coconut on a baking sheet, and toast for 10 to 12 minutes, stirring occasionally, or until flakes are lightly browned. Remove coconut from the oven, and set aside. Turn off the oven.

2. Combine butter, sugar, lemon zest, and lemon oil in a mixing bowl, and beat at low speed with an electric mixer to blend. Increase the speed to high, and beat for 3 to 4 minutes, or until light and fluffy. Slowly add flour and salt to the butter mixture, and beat until soft dough forms. Beat in cooled coconut.

3. Place dough on a sheet of waxed paper, and form it into a log 2½ inches in diameter. Refrigerate dough covered in plastic wrap for 2 hours, or until firm, or up to 2 days.

4. Preheat the oven to 350°F. Line two baking sheets with parchment paper or silicon baking mats.

5. Cut chilled dough into ¼-inch slices using a sharp serrated knife, and arrange them on the baking sheets. Decorate cookies with sugar crystals, if using.

6. Bake cookies for 10 to 12 minutes, or until edges are brown. Cool cookies for 2 minutes on the baking sheets, and then transfer cookies to racks to cool completely.

7. For filling, combine confectioners' sugar, butter, lemon zest, lemon juice, and corn syrup in a mixing bowl, and beat at low speed with an electric mixer to combine. Increase the speed to high, and beat for 2 to 3 minutes, or until light and fluffy. Place 1 teaspoon of filling on the flat side of half of cookies, and top with the flat side of another cookie. Refrigerate cookies for 15 minutes to firm filling.

NOTE: Keep unfilled cookies in an airtight container, layered between sheets of waxed paper or parchment, at room temperature for up to 5 days.

VARIATION:

• Substitute lime zest and lime oil for the lemon zest and lemon oil.

✻ ✻

If you're in a hurry to begin a batter you can grate the butter through the large holes of a box grater. But do not soften butter in a microwave oven. It will become too soft.

✻ ✻

HASHED UP HONEY NUT COOKIES

Honey is a great flavor any time of year, and it's usually competing with lots of spices and gets lost. But not so with this refrigerator cookie! It's the star, and the nuts add more interest too.

YIELD: 5 dozen
ACTIVE TIME: 25 minutes
START TO FINISH: 2¾ hours, including 2 hours to chill dough

1 cup finely chopped walnuts or pecans
½ cup honey
½ cup firmly packed dark brown sugar
½ cup (8 tablespoons) Bong Butter (page 23), softened
1 large egg, at room temperature
½ teaspoon pure vanilla extract

1 teaspoon baking powder
¼ teaspoon baking soda
½ teaspoon salt
2½ cups all-purpose flour
Royal Icing (page 36), optional
Confectioners' Sugar Glaze (page 34), optional

1. Preheat the oven to 350°F. Place nuts on a baking sheet, and toast for 5 to 7 minutes, or until browned. Remove nuts from the oven, and set aside. Turn off the oven.

2. Combine honey, brown sugar, and butter in a mixing bowl, and beat at low speed with an electric mixer to blend. Increase the speed to high, and beat for 3 to 4 minutes, or until light and fluffy. Beat in egg, vanilla, baking powder, baking soda, and salt and beat for 1 minute. Slowly add flour to butter mixture, and beat until soft dough forms. Fold in nuts.

3. Place dough on a sheet of waxed paper, and form it into a log 2½ inches in diameter. Refrigerate dough covered in plastic wrap for 2 hours, or until firm, or up to 2 days.

4. Preheat the oven to 350°F. Line two baking sheets with parchment paper or silicon baking mats.

5. Cut chilled dough into ¼-inch slices using a sharp serrated knife, and arrange them on the baking sheets.

6. Bake cookies for 10 to 12 minutes, or until edges are brown. Cool cookies for 2 minutes on the baking sheets, and then transfer cookies to racks to cool completely. Decorate cookies with Royal Icing or Confectioners' Sugar Glaze, if using.

NOTE: Keep cookies in an airtight container, layered between sheets of waxed paper or parchment, at room temperature for up to 5 days. Cookies can also be frozen for up to 2 months.

Baking powder does not live forever, and if you haven't used it in a while try this test: Mix 2 teaspoons of baking powder with 1 cup of hot tap water. If there's an immediate reaction of fizzing and foaming, the baking powder can be used. If the reaction is at all delayed or weak, throw the baking powder away and buy a fresh can.

☘ MINTY GRASSHOPPER CHOCOLATE SANDWICH COOKIES

Mint and chocolate is a great combo, especially when there's some whacky weed in both the crispy cookies and creamy white chocolate filling. These are an adult version of that Girl Scout cookie we loved as kids.

YIELD: 3 dozen

ACTIVE TIME: 25 minutes

START TO FINISH: 3 hours, including 2 hours to chill dough

Cookies

1 cup (16 tablespoons) Bong Butter (page 23), softened

¾ cup granulated sugar

1 large egg yolk, at room temperature

½ teaspoon pure vanilla extract

½ teaspoon baking powder

½ teaspoon salt

½ cup unsweetened cocoa powder

2 cups all-purpose flour

Filling

½ cup heavy cream

1½ tablespoons light corn syrup

¾ pound fine-quality white chocolate, finely chopped

2 tablespoons Bong Butter (page 23), softened

1 teaspoon mint oil or mint extract

¼ teaspoon red or green food coloring, optional

Royal Icing (page 36), optional

Confectioners' Sugar Glaze (page 34), optional

1. Combine butter and sugar in a mixing bowl, and beat at low speed with an electric mixer to blend. Increase the speed to high, and beat for 3 to 4 minutes, or until light and fluffy. Beat in egg yolk, vanilla, baking powder, and salt, and beat for 1 minute. Slowly add cocoa and flour to butter mixture, and beat until stiff dough forms.

2. Place dough on a sheet of waxed paper, and form it into a log 2½ inches in diameter. Refrigerate dough covered in plastic wrap for 2 hours, or until firm, or up to 2 days.

3. While dough chills, prepare filling. Bring cream and corn syrup just to a simmer in a small saucepan. Stir in chocolate, butter, and mint oil, and cover the pan, and remove the pan from the heat. Allow mixture to sit for 5 minutes, then stir well, and stir in food coloring, if using. Heat over very low heat if chocolate still has lumps. Press a sheet of waxed paper into the surface of filling, and refrigerate.

4. Preheat the oven to 350°F. Line two baking sheets with parchment paper or silicon baking mats.

5. Cut chilled dough into ⅓-inch slices using a sharp serrated knife, and arrange them on the baking sheets. Decorate cookies with sugar crystals.

6. Bake cookies for 10 to 12 minutes, or until edges are brown. Cool cookies for 2 minutes on the baking sheets, and then transfer cookies to racks to cool completely.

7. Beat filling with an electric mixer on medium speed for 2 minutes, or until light and fluffy. Place a dollop of filling on the flat side of 1 cookie, and top with the flat side of another cookie. Chill for at least 1 hour, or until filling is set. Decorate cookies with Royal Icing or Confectioners' Sugar Glaze, if using.

NOTE: Keep cookies refrigerated in an airtight container, layered between sheets of waxed paper or parchment, for up to 5 days.

VARIATIONS:

• Substitute rum extract for the mint oil and omit the food coloring.

• Add 1 tablespoon instant espresso powder dissolved in 2 tablespoons boiling water to the dough, and substitute pure vanilla extract for the mint oil.

❋ ❋

One of the additional health benefits of chocolate is that it has been found to contain catechins—some of the same antioxidants found in green tea. The catechins attack free radicals that damage cells and are thought to lead to cancer and heart disease. Therefore, eating chocolate may help to prevent heart disease and cancer—as long as it's eaten in small quantities.

❋ ❋

✳ CHOCOLATE CANDY REEFER REFRIGERATOR COOKIES

It can be difficult to make chocolate chip cookies really uniform and crispy because the chips are integrated into the dough. But not true in this case. The miniature chips are on top!

YIELD: 3 dozen cookies
ACTIVE TIME: 15 minutes
START TO FINISH: 2½ hours, including 2 hours to chill dough

¾ cup (12 tablespoons) Bong Butter (page 23), softened
½ cup granulated sugar
¾ teaspoon pure vanilla extract
2 large egg yolks, at room temperature
1¾ cups all-purpose flour
1½ cups miniature chocolate chips

1. Combine butter, sugar, and vanilla in a mixing bowl, and beat at medium speed with an electric mixer to blend. Increase the speed to high, and beat until light and fluffy. Reduce the speed to medium and add egg yolks, beating well, and scraping the sides of the bowl as necessary. Reduce the speed to low, and add flour.

2. Scrape dough onto a floured counter, and divide it in half. Roll each ½ into a log 2 inches in diameter. Wrap logs in plastic wrap for 2 hours, or until chilled and firm.

3. Preheat the oven to 350°F and grease two cookie sheets or line them with silicon baking mats. Slice logs into ⅓-inch slices, and place them 1 inch apart on the prepared baking sheets. Pat chocolate chips into tops of cookies.

4. Bake cookies for 12 to 15 minutes, or until edges are lightly browned. Remove the cookies from the oven and transfer to racks to cool completely.

NOTE: The cookies can be made up to 5 days in advance and kept at room temperature in an airtight container. Also, the logs can be refrigerated for up to 3 days or frozen for up to 3 months.

VARIATION:

Substitute orange oil for the vanilla extract and add 1 tablespoon grated orange zest to the dough.

✻✻

The chocolate chip cookie was developed in 1930 by Ruth Graves Wakefield, owner of the Toll House Inn in Whitman, Massachusetts. The restaurant's popularity was not just due to its home-cooked style meals. Ruth's policy was to give diners a whole extra helping of their entrées to take home with them and a serving of her homemade cookies for dessert.

✻✻

CHAPTER 4

. . . .

One-Pan Wonders: Bar Cookies

There's no question that bar cookies are the quickest and easiest cookies to make. After the batter or dough is mixed it's baked in one pan, and then cut into pieces. You're done. How many cookies each batch makes depends on how large the pieces are that you cut, and for Christmas when you're baking any number of different cookies, I suggest making the bars no more than 1½-inch pieces.

There's no need to spend time chilling the dough because it's not going to be rolled, and there's no need to take the time to form individual portions as you do for drop cookies. On the flip side, bar cookie recipes do require a longer baking time. But while they're in the oven you can be trimming your tree or chewing on other cheeba treats.

A subset of bar cookies is ever-popular brownies and their first cousin, blondies. You'll find a good range of those recipes in this chapter too.

One downside of bar cookies at Christmas, however, is that they usually don't have the visual appeal of decorated sugar cookies or whimsical gingerbread people. My suggestion is to cut them into very small bites and present them in small paper cups as miniatures. This approach also increases the batch size from 12 or 16 larger cookies to at least 2 dozen.

Another way to dress them up is by cutting them into shapes other than squares and rectangles. Diamond-shaped cookies are pretty, and if you cut the bars with a round biscuit cutter you have all the tiny bits between the cookies as a treat for the cook!

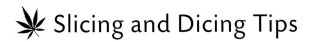

🌿 Slicing and Dicing Tips

How and when you cut bar cookies depends on the recipe. With most you allow the pan to cool completely on a wire cooling rack, and then cut them, but there are also recipes that benefit from being chilled before being sliced.

A sharp, serrated knife is the best tool to use, although the knife can damage the pan. Lining the baking pan with heavy-duty aluminum foil, allow the foil to come up high enough so that you can bend it over, which makes it possible to remove the bar cookies from the pan and cut them on a cutting board. It also means you don't have a pan to wash. Line the pan, pressing the foil into all the crevices and edges, and then treat it as dictated in the recipe, either just greased or greased and dusted with flour.

The key to successful slicing is the word *slowly*—especially if you're stoned. If you cut cookies too quickly it can cause the edges to fracture and you're left with crumbs instead of slices.

If slicing them in the pan, begin by creating space in the pan by removing the four edges, which are never as attractive. Cut around about ½-inch into the pan, and then remove those thin slices and consider them a treat. Then work from alternate sides. Depending on the cookie, it's frequently easier to cut a long slice and then divide it out of the pan.

Alternate tools for successfully slicing bar cookies are a curved pizza rocker or a traditional pizza wheel. Use the wheel only on thin cookies; the rounded edge of the rocker makes it perfect for all cookies.

ATOMIC ALL ABOUT ALMOND BARS

Almond paste gives these dense and chewy cookies an intense almond flavor, balanced by the crunch provided by the almonds on the top.

YIELD: 2 to 3 dozen
ACTIVE TIME: 15 minutes
START TO FINISH: 1 hour

1¼ cups all-purpose flour
¾ cup confectioners' sugar
½ teaspoon baking soda
¼ teaspoon salt
¾ cup (12 tablespoons) Bong Butter (page 23), sliced
⅔ cup firmly packed almond paste
1 large egg, at room temperature
1 tablespoon whole milk
1 teaspoon pure almond extract
1 large egg white
1 cup sliced almonds

1. Preheat the oven to 350°F. Grease a 9 x 9-inch baking pan.

2. Combine flour, confectioners' sugar, baking soda, and salt in a food processor fitted with the steel blade. Blend for 5 seconds. Add butter and almond paste to the work bowl, and process until mixture resembles coarse meal.

3. Combine egg, milk, almond extract in a small cup, and whisk well. Drizzle liquid into the work bowl, and pulse about 10 times, or until stiff dough forms. If dough is dry and doesn't come together, add additional milk by 1-teaspoon amounts, until dough forms a ball.

4. Press dough into the prepared pan. Whisk egg white in a small cup and spread over dough. Pat almonds evenly onto dough.

5. Bake for 35 to 40 minutes or until top is golden. Cool completely in the pan on a cooling rack, then cut into bars.

NOTE: Keep cookies in an airtight container, layered between sheets of waxed paper or parchment, at room temperature for up to 5 days. Cookies can also be frozen for up to 2 months.

VARIATION:

• Substitute chocolate chips for the almonds, and omit the egg white.

✳ ✳

When shopping for this recipe, make sure you buy almond paste, not marzipan. They usually have them right next to each other on the shelf. Both have almond flavor, but marzipan already has sugar added.

✳ ✳

CARAMEL PECAN BAMBA BARS

These rich and gooey cookies are like a pecan pie you can hold with your fingers. The crispy cookie crust supports all sorts of crunchy and creamy elements in the topping.

YIELD: 2 to 3 dozen
ACTIVE TIME: 20 minutes
START TO FINISH: 1 hour

½ pound pecan halves
1 cup all-purpose flour
⅓ cup confectioners' sugar
¼ teaspoon salt
1 cup (16 tablespoons) Bong Butter
(page 23), divided

1 large egg, at room temperature
½ teaspoon pure vanilla extract
¼ teaspoon pure almond extract
¾ cup firmly packed light brown sugar
¼ cup light corn syrup
¼ cup heavy cream

1. Preheat the oven to 375°F. Line a 9 x 9-inch baking pan with heavy-duty aluminum foil, allowing the sides to be long and wrapped around the sides of the pan. Grease the foil. Place pecans on a baking sheet, and toast for 5 to 7 minutes, or until lightly browned.

2. Combine flour, confectioners' sugar, and salt in a food processor fitted with the steel blade. Blend for 5 seconds. Add 8 tablespoons of butter to the work bowl, and process, using on-and-off pulsing, until mixture resembles coarse meal.

3. Combine egg, vanilla, and almond extract in a small cup, and whisk well. Drizzle liquid into the work bowl, and pulse about 10 times, or until stiff dough forms. If dough is dry and doesn't come together, add milk by 1-teaspoon amounts, until dough forms a ball.

4. Transfer dough to prepared pan. Using floured fingers and an offset spatula, press dough firmly into the bottom and ¾-inch up sides. Freeze until firm, about 15 minutes. Prick dough on the bottom of the pan with the tines of a fork. Bake crust for 10 to 12 minutes, or until lightly browned.

5. While crust bakes, prepare topping. Combine remaining butter, brown sugar, and corn syrup in a saucepan, and bring to a boil over high heat, whisking constantly. Boil for 2 minutes. Remove the pan from the heat, and stir in cream and pecans.

6. Spoon topping over crust, smoothing the top with a spatula. Bake for 20 to 22 minutes, or until topping is bubbling and dark brown. Cool completely in the pan on a cooling rack. Remove cookies from the pan by pulling up on the sides of the foil, and cut into bars.

NOTE: Keep cookies in an airtight container, layered between sheets of waxed paper or parchment, at room temperature for up to 5 days.

VARIATIONS:

- Substitute maple sugar for the light brown sugar, substitute pure maple syrup for the corn syrup, and substitute walnuts for the pecans.
- Add ½ cup dried currants to the topping.

Like many recipes for pre-baked piecrust, the crust in this recipe is pricked with a fork to prevent shrinkage while it bakes. The dough has a tendency to shrink when it is heated in the oven and the liquid evaporates.

✹ AUNT MARY'S WHITE CHOCOLATE ALMOND SQUARES

These tantalizing treats are a monochromatic contrast to most Christmas cookies, which makes them really stand out. Chopped toasted almonds top a layer of angelic white chocolate.

YIELD: 4 dozen
ACTIVE TIME: 15 minutes
START TO FINISH: 45 minutes

1 cup chopped blanched almonds
1 cup (16 tablespoons) Bong Butter (page 23), softened
1 cup firmly packed dark brown sugar
1 large egg yolk, at room temperature
1 teaspoon pure vanilla extract
2 cups all-purpose flour
¼ teaspoon salt
½ pound good-quality white chocolate, chopped

1. Preheat the oven to 350°F. Line a 9 x 13-inch baking pan with parchment paper. Place almonds on a baking sheet, and toast for 5 to 7 minutes, or until lightly browned.

2. Combine butter and sugar in a mixing bowl, and beat at low speed with an electric mixer to blend. Increase the speed to high, and beat for 3 to 4 minutes, or until light and fluffy. Beat in egg yolk and vanilla, and beat for 1 minute. Slowly add flour and salt to the butter mixture, and beat until stiff dough forms. Pat dough evenly into the bottom of the pan, and prick it with the tines of a fork.

3. Bake crust in the center of the oven for 20 minutes, or until light brown.

4. Remove the pan from the oven and scatter chocolate evenly over crust. Return the pan to the oven for 1 minute. Remove the pan again and spread the chocolate evenly over the crust. Sprinkle evenly with the almonds.

5. Cool completely in the pan on a cooling rack, then cut into bars.

NOTE: Keep cookies in an airtight container, layered between sheets of waxed paper or parchment, at room temperature for up to 5 days.

VARIATION:
• Substitute maple sugar for the brown sugar, and substitute walnuts for almonds.

✻ ✻

Here's a great factoid to wow your friends. Botanically-speaking, almonds are a fruit. On the tree, the fruit or drupe looks like a small, elongated peach with a hard greenish-gray husk. When mature, the husk splits open to reveal the shell that in turn contains the nutmeat. Spanish missionaries are credited for bringing the almond to California, now the world's largest producer of more than 100 varieties of almonds.

✻ ✻

WHITE CHOCOLATE TWISTED PEPPERMINT SHORTBREADS

There's aromatic mint oil in the cookie base of these easy-to-make yummies, and then the minty freshness is reinforced by a pretty sprinkling of crushed red-and-white candies on top.

YIELD: 3 dozen
ACTIVE TIME: 15 minutes
START TO FINISH: 50 minutes

1 cup (16 tablespoons) Bong Butter (page 23), softened
1 cup granulated sugar
1 large egg, at room temperature
½ teaspoon peppermint oil or pure peppermint extract
½ teaspoon pure vanilla extract
2 cups all-purpose flour
¼ teaspoon salt
10 ounces white chocolate, finely chopped
¾ cup crushed red and white peppermint candies

1. Preheat the oven to 350°F. Line a 9 x 13-inch baking pan with heavy-duty aluminum foil, allowing the sides to be long and wrapped around the sides of the pan. Grease the foil.

2. Combine butter and sugar in a mixing bowl, and beat at low speed with an electric mixer to blend. Increase the speed to high, and beat for 3 to 4 minutes, or until light and fluffy. Beat in egg, peppermint oil, and vanilla, and beat for 1 minute. Slowly add flour and salt to the butter mixture, and beat until stiff dough forms. Pat dough evenly into the bottom of the pan, and prick it with the tines of a fork.

3. Bake crust in the center of the oven for 20 to 25 minutes, or until light brown.

4. Remove the pan from the oven and scatter chocolate evenly over crust. Return the pan to the oven for 1 minute. Remove the pan again and spread chocolate evenly over the crust. Sprinkle evenly with crushed candy.

5. Cool completely in the pan on a cooling rack. Remove cookies from the pan using the foil, and cut into bars.

NOTE: Keep cookies in an airtight container, layered between sheets of waxed paper or parchment, at room temperature for up to 5 days.

VARIATIONS:

- Omit the peppermint extract, and substitute chopped toffee bits for the peppermint candy.
- Substitute dark chocolate for the white chocolate.

✸✸✸

Actually ivory in color, white chocolate is technically not chocolate at all; it is made from cocoa butter, sugar, and flavoring. It is difficult to work with, and should be used only in recipes that are specifically designed for it. Dark chocolate can be substituted for white chocolate, but white chocolate cannot be substituted for dark chocolate.

✸✸✸

LOCO WEED LEMON SQUARES

This is a great last-minute recipe since most of us have a lemon or two in the house, along with basic baking ingredients.

YIELD: 2 to 3 dozen
ACTIVE TIME: 10 minutes
START TO FINISH: 50 minutes

½ cup (8 tablespoons) Bong Butter (page 23), melted
⅓ cup confectioners' sugar, divided
1 cup plus 2 tablespoons all-purpose flour
Pinch of salt

2 large eggs, at room temperature
1 cup granulated sugar
⅓ cup freshly squeezed lemon juice
1 tablespoon grated lemon zest

1. Preheat the oven to 350°F, and grease the bottom and sides of an 8 x 8-inch baking pan.

2. Combine butter, ¼ cup confectioners' sugar, 1 cup flour, and salt in a mixing bowl, and mix thoroughly. Press mixture into the prepared pan. Bake for 20 minutes or until set and lightly brown. Remove crust from the oven, and set aside.

3. Combine eggs, granulated sugar, remaining 2 tablespoons flour, lemon juice, and lemon zest in a mixing bowl. Beat with an electric mixer on medium speed for 1 minute, or until well blended. Pour topping over crust, and bake for 20 minutes, or until barely brown. The custard should still be soft. Cool the pan on a cooling rack, then cut into bars.

VARIATION:

• Substitute lime juice and lime zest for the lemon juice and lemon zest.

✳ ✳

The easiest way to get the most juice out of lemons or limes is to have the fruit at room temperature and roll it around on a counter a few times before cutting it in half. If you need just a few tablespoons of juice, squeeze the juice through the fingers of your other hand. That way you can catch and discard the seeds.

✳ ✳

CHEEBA CHOCOLATE COCONUT BARS

I really groove out on those candy bars that are chocolate-covered coconut, so I decided to turn them into a cookie bar with that special ingredient that makes them ever so much tastier for a few hours.

YIELD: 3 to 4 dozen
ACTIVE TIME: 10 minutes
START TO FINISH: 35 minutes

1 cup (16 tablespoons) Bong Butter (page 23)
¾ cup granulated sugar
¾ cup firmly packed light brown sugar
2 large eggs, at room temperature
1 teaspoon pure almond extract
¼ cup unsweetened cocoa powder
1 teaspoon baking soda
½ teaspoon salt
2 cups all-purpose flour
1 cup miniature chocolate chips
1 (14-ounce) can sweetened condensed milk
1 cup firmly packed unsweetened coconut flakes

1. Preheat the oven to 375°F, and grease a 9 x 13-inch baking pan.

2. Combine butter, granulated sugar, and brown sugar in a mixing bowl, and beat at low speed with an electric mixer to blend. Increase the speed to high, and beat for 3 to 4 minutes, or until light and fluffy. Beat in eggs, and almond extract, and beat well again.

3. Beat in cocoa powder, baking soda, and salt at medium speed. Reduce the speed to low, and add flour. Fold in chocolate chips.

4. Spread batter into the prepared pan. Combine condensed milk and coconut in a small bowl, and stir well. Spread as an even layer on top of chocolate dough.

5. Bake for 25 to 30 minutes, or until a toothpick inserted comes out clean. Cool the pan on a cooling rack, and then cut into bars.

NOTE: Keep cookies in an airtight container, layered between sheets of waxed paper or parchment, at room temperature for up to 5 days. Cookies can also be frozen for up to 2 months.

✳✳

The Aztecs first discovered chocolate, and our word comes from the Aztec xocolatl, which means "bitter water." Famed King Montezuma believed chocolate was an aphrodisiac and is reported to have consumed some 50 cups a day.

✳✳✳✳✳✳✳✳✳✳✳✳✳✳✳✳✳✳✳✳✳✳✳✳✳✳✳✳✳✳✳✳✳✳✳✳

❋LAYERED CHIRA CHIP AND COCONUT BARS

These bars are as much a Christmas classic as "The Nutcracker." But in this version there's a nice buzz too. The base is like a cookie with creamy topping with chips and coconut as a crown.

YIELD: 2 to 3 dozen

ACTIVE TIME: 15 minutes

START TO FINISH: 1 hour

1 cup coarsely chopped pecans

1 cup graham cracker crumbs

½ cup rolled oats

½ cup (8 tablespoons) Bong Butter (page 23), melted and cooled

1 (14-ounce) can sweetened condensed milk

1 cup bittersweet chocolate chips

1 cup chopped walnuts

1 cup shredded coconut

1. Preheat the oven to 350°F, and grease a 9 x 9- inch baking pan. Place pecans on a baking sheet, and toast for 5 to 7 minutes, or until lightly browned.

2. Combine nuts, graham cracker crumbs, oats, and butter in a mixing bowl. Mix well. Pat mixture into the prepared pan.

3. Pour sweetened condensed milk over crust, and spread into an even layer. Sprinkle chocolate chips and walnuts over milk, and then top with coconut. Press topping down lightly with your fingers or the back of a spoon.

4. Bake for 25 to 30 minutes or until coconut is brown. Cool completely in the pan on a cooling rack, then cut into bars.

NOTE: Keep cookies in an airtight container, layered between sheets of waxed paper or parchment, at room temperature for up to 5 days.

VARIATION:
• Substitute 1 cup chopped dried fruit or raisins for 1 cup of the chips.

✳ ✳

Born in 1801, Gail Borden Jr. was the American inventor of condensed milk in 1856, although a similar product had appeared a few years earlier in England. Borden insisted that farmers who wanted to sell him raw milk had to keep their facilities and their cows clean and sanitary. By 1858, Borden's milk, sold as Eagle Brand, had gained a reputation for purity, durability, and economy.

✳ ✳

✿ VIXEN'S CHOCOLATE PEPPERMINT BROWNIES

These brownies with a double dose of chocolate are topped with a creamy peppermint frosting, and then made even prettier with some crushed candies.

YIELD: 2 to 3 dozen miniatures
ACTIVE TIME: 15 minutes
START TO FINISH: 1 hour

3 ounces bittersweet chocolate, chopped

⅓ cup heavy cream, divided

1 cup all-purpose flour

3 tablespoons unsweetened cocoa powder

½ teaspoon salt

¾ cup (12 tablespoons) Bong Butter (page 23), softened, divided

2½ cups confectioners' sugar, divided

2 large eggs

½ teaspoon pure vanilla extract

½ to 1 teaspoon mint oil

2 to 4 drops red food coloring (optional)

¾ cup crushed red-and-white peppermint candies

1. Preheat the oven to 350°F, and grease a 9 x 9-inch baking pan. Combine chocolate and 2 tablespoons cream in a microwave safe bowl. Microwave on Medium (50 percent power) at 30 second intervals, stirring between intervals, until chocolate is melted and smooth. Set aside.

2. Combine flour, cocoa powder, and salt in a mixing bowl. Whisk well.

3. Combine 8 tablespoons butter and ½ cup sugar in another mixing bowl and beat at low speed with an electric mixer to blend. Increase the speed to high, and beat for 3 to 4 minutes, or until light and fluffy. Add eggs, one at a time, and beat well between each addition. Beat in cooled chocolate and vanilla. Slowly add dry ingredients to the butter mixture, and beat until dough forms.

4. Scrape batter into the prepared pan, and spread evenly. Bake for 15 minutes, or until firm and a toothpick inserted into the center comes out clean. Cool completely in the pan on a cooling rack.

5. For frosting, combine remaining butter and remaining sugar in a mixing bowl, and add 2 tablespoons of the remaining cream. Beat at medium speed with an electric mixer until light and fluffy. Add mint oil and red food coloring, if using, and beat well. Add additional cream by 1-teaspoon amounts if frosting is too thick to spread.

6. Spread frosting over brownies, and sprinkle crushed candies evenly over frosting. Cut into small bars.

NOTE: Keep brownies in an airtight container, layered between sheets of waxed paper or parchment, at room temperature for up to 5 days.

VARIATION:

• For chocolate almond brownies, substitute pure almond extract for the mint oil, omit the food coloring, and substitute slivered almonds (toasted in a 350°F oven for 7 to 9 minutes) for the peppermint candies.

Because chocolate can absorb aromas and flavors from other foods, it should always be wrapped tightly after being opened. Store chocolate in a cool, dry place, but it should not be refrigerated or frozen. If stored at a high temperature, the fat will rise to the surface and become a whitish powder called a bloom. It will disappear, however, as soon as the chocolate is melted.

ALICE B. TOKLAS WHITE CHOCOLATE MARBLE BROWNIES

No book containing cheeba creations should be published without a recipe for a boosted brownie! I adore the combination of white chocolate and cream cheese, and these brownies deliver both.

YIELD: 3 to 4 dozen
ACTIVE TIME: 15 minutes
START TO FINISH: 1 hour

½ cup (8 tablespoons) Bong Butter (page 23)
4 ounces white chocolate, chopped
3 large eggs, at room temperature, divided
1 cup granulated sugar, divided
½ cup all-purpose flour
Pinch of salt
1 (8-ounce) package cream cheese, softened
½ teaspoon pure vanilla extract
¼ teaspoon red or green food coloring

1. Preheat the oven to 350°F. Grease and flour a 9 x 9-inch baking pan.

2. Melt butter and white chocolate over low heat or in a microwave oven. Stir to combine, and set aside for 5 minutes to cool.

3. Combine 2 eggs and ¾ cup sugar in mixing bowl. Beat with an electric mixer on medium speed for 1 minute, or until well combined. Add cooled chocolate mixture, and beat for 1 minute. Add flour and salt and beat at low speed until just blended.

4. In another bowl, combine cream cheese, remaining ¼ cup sugar, remaining 1 egg, vanilla, and food coloring. Beat with an electric mixer on medium speed for 2 minutes, or until light and fluffy. Spread batter into the prepared pan. Top with cream cheese batter and swirl layers together with a fork.

5. Bake for 35 minutes or until the top is springy to the touch. Cool the pan on a cooling rack, then cut into bars.

NOTE: The brownies can be made up to 3 days in advance and kept at room temperature, tightly covered with plastic wrap. They also freeze well for up to 1 month, so make a double batch.

Alice Babette Toklas, a native of San Francisco, met Gertrude Stein the first day she arrived in Paris in 1907. She was Stein's confidante and lover, as well as partner in her famous soirees, until Stein's death in 1946. Stein published her own memoirs with the title The Autobiography of Alice B. Toklas in 1933, but the recipe for hash-laced brownies was part of Alice's own book, The Alice B. Toklas Cookbook, which was published in 1954.

✺ PEANUT BUTTER AND CHOCOLATE LAYERED BOOM-BOOM BROWNIES

These chocolate brownies are topped with a layer of peanut butter frosting, which is then coated with even more chocolate for a sinfully rich and delicious treat. It's like a cookie version of a Reese's peanut butter cup.

YIELD: 3 to 4 dozen
ACTIVE TIME: 25 minutes
START TO FINISH: 2 hours

1½ cups (24 tablespoons) Bong Butter (page 23), softened, divided
14 ounces bittersweet chocolate, chopped, divided
3 ounces unsweetened chocolate, chopped
1½ cups granulated sugar
1½ teaspoons pure vanilla extract, divided
4 large eggs, at room temperature
1 cup all-purpose flour
1 cup roasted salted peanuts, coarsely chopped
1 cup chunky commercial peanut butter (do not use natural)
¾ cup confectioners' sugar
⅛ teaspoon salt
1 tablespoon whole milk

1. Preheat the oven to 325°F. Line a 9 x 13-inch baking pan with heavy-duty aluminum foil, allowing the sides to be long and wrapped around the sides of the pan. Grease the foil.

2. Melt ¾ cup butter, 7 ounces of bittersweet chocolate, and unsweetened chocolate in a heavy saucepan over low heat, stirring frequently until the mixture is melted and smooth. Remove the pan from the heat, and set aside for 5 to 7 minutes to cool. This can also be done in a microwave.

3. Whisk sugar, 1 teaspoon vanilla, and salt, then eggs, 1 at a time into cooled chocolate. Whisk in flour, and stir in peanuts. Spread batter evenly in the prepared pan.

4. Bake for 30 minutes, or until a toothpick inserted into the center comes out with moist crumbs attached. Cool completely in the pan on a cooling rack.

5. Combine peanut butter and 4 tablespoons of remaining butter in a mixing bowl, and beat at low speed with an electric mixer to blend. Add confectioners' sugar, salt, milk, and remaining ½ teaspoon vanilla, and beat for 2 minutes, or until light and fluffy. Spread mixture on top of brownies, and chill brownies for 1 hour.

6. Combine remaining chocolate and remaining butter in a small saucepan, and melt over low heat. Stir until smooth. Place dollops of chocolate on top of peanut butter layer, and spread gently to cover peanut butter layer completely.

7. Chill brownies, lightly covered with plastic wrap, for at least 1 hour, or until chocolate is firm. Remove brownies from the pan by pulling up on the sides of the foil, and then cut into bars. Bring brownies to room temperature before serving.

NOTE: Keep brownies in an airtight container, layered between sheets of waxed paper or parchment, refrigerated, for up to 3 days.

✳✳✳✳✳✳✳✳✳✳✳✳✳✳✳✳✳✳✳✳✳✳✳✳✳✳✳✳✳

Peanuts are used in cuisines around the world, but peanut butter is a home-grown American invention. It was developed in 1890 and first promoted as a health food at the 1904 World's Fair in St. Louis.

✳✳✳✳✳✳✳✳✳✳✳✳✳✳✳✳✳✳✳✳✳✳✳✳✳✳✳✳✳

George Washington Carver, an educator at the Tuskegee Institute in Alabama, was an avid promoter of peanuts as a replacement for the region's cotton crop, which had been severely damaged by the boll weevil. In his 1916 Research Bulletin called How to Grow the Peanut and 105 Ways of Preparing it for Human Consumption, he included three recipes for peanut cookies calling for crushed/chopped peanuts as an ingredient. It was not until the early 1920s that peanut butter is listed as an ingredient in the cookies.

CHRISTMAS BLONDIES

While blondies are the name given to brownie-like cookies made without chocolate, these blondies are laced with blonde, so you'll really get off on their heady flavor. Chopped pistachios and dried cranberries add the seasonal colors too.

YIELD: 3 to 4 dozen
ACTIVE TIME: 15 minutes
START TO FINISH: 50 minutes

¾ cup (12 tablespoons) Bong Butter (page 23)
1½ cups firmly packed light brown sugar
2 large eggs, at room temperature
½ teaspoon pure vanilla extract
1½ teaspoons baking powder
½ teaspoon salt
2⅓ cups all-purpose flour
¾ cup dried cranberries
¾ cup chopped pistachio nuts

1. Preheat the oven to 350°F, and grease a 9 x 13-inch baking pan.

2. Combine butter and sugar in a saucepan. Place over medium heat and cook, stirring frequently, until butter melts and mixture is smooth. Scrape mixture into a mixing bowl. Cool to room temperature.

3. Whisk eggs and vanilla into mixture, beating until smooth. Beat in baking powder and salt, and then flour. Fold in dried cranberries and pistachio nuts.

4. Scrape batter into the pan, and bake for 20 minutes, or until a toothpick inserted in the center comes out clean. Cool the pan on a cooling rack, and then cut into bars.

NOTE: Keep cookies in an airtight container, layered between sheets of waxed paper or parchment, at room temperature for up to 5 days. Cookies can also be frozen for up to 2 months.

VARIATIONS:

- Substitute dried cherries or chopped dried strawberries for the dried cranberries.
- Substitute almond extract for the vanilla extract.

✳ ✳

Brown sugar is granulated sugar mixed with molasses, and the darker the color, the more pronounced the molasses flavor. If a recipe calls for dark brown sugar and you only have light brown sugar, add 2 tablespoons molasses per ½ cup sugar to replicate the taste.

✳ ✳

CHAPTER 5

....

Piles of Perfection: Drop Cookies

The weed-filled wonders in this chapter fall somewhere between rolled cookies and bar cookies on the labor scale. They're more work than bars but far less than rolled cookies. Plus they don't need to be decorated afterward so they can go straight from the baking sheet to the baker's mouth. Although these cookies don't have a holiday theme, the category includes some perennial favorites that make every day a holiday. And these are the cookies that people always want to swap, at Christmas or any day.

The word *drop* is a misnomer. The dough doesn't really drop onto the baking sheets without some coaxing. But we won't start now calling them "coaxed cookies" just for the sake of accuracy.

There are two ways to accomplish this task: another spoon or a finger. If using the "two spoon method," spray both spoons with vegetable oil spray first to make it easier to slide the dough off with the other spoon. The success of drop cookies depends on mounds of a uniform size. The size not only includes the diameter of the circle but also its height.

Here are some other tips for making drop cookies:

- Cool your cookie sheets by running the back under cold water between batches. Placing dough on a warm cookie sheet makes the cookies flatten.

- Take note of how far apart the mounds of cookie dough should be placed on the baking sheet. Some cookies spread far more than others.

- Rotate the cookie sheets midway through the baking time if using two sheets. Even if baking with a convection fan, cookies on an upper rack brown more quickly than those on a lower rack.

- Always allow cookies to cool for 2 minutes on the baking sheets before transferring them to cooling racks.

If the cookies are of a uniform size, the difference between chewy cookies and crisp cookies is the baking time. All these recipes have a range given of a few minutes. If you bake them for the minimum amount of time, you'll have a much moister and chewier cookie than if you let them go for the full baking time at which point much of the moisture will have evaporated.

CRUNCHY PEANUT BUTTER AND GOBLETS OF JAM THUMBPRINTS

It's fun to make thumbprint cookies. You get to poke the dough, and then you get to fill the indentation with something fun. These cookies give you some good crunchy texture too.

YIELD: 3 dozen
ACTIVE TIME: 20 minutes
START TO FINISH: 45 minutes

¾ cup firmly packed light brown sugar
½ cup (8 tablespoons) Bong Butter (page 23), softened
1 cup smooth commercial peanut butter (not homemade or natural)
1 large egg, at room temperature
½ teaspoon pure vanilla extract (2 grams)
1 teaspoon baking soda
⅛ teaspoon salt
1 cup all-purpose flour
1 cup finely chopped roasted peanuts
1½ cups seedless raspberry jam

1. Preheat the oven to 375°F. Line two baking sheets with parchment paper or silicon baking mats.

2. Combine brown sugar, butter, and peanut butter in a mixing bowl, and beat at low speed with an electric mixer to blend. Increase the speed to high, and beat for 3 to 4 minutes, or until light and fluffy. Beat in egg, vanilla, baking soda, and salt and beat for 1 minute. Slowly add flour to the butter mixture, and beat until soft dough forms.

3. Roll dough in scant 1-tablespoon portions into balls, and roll balls in chopped peanuts. Place balls 1½ inches apart on the baking sheets, and make a large depression with your index finger in the center of each ball.

4. Bake cookies for 10 to 12 minutes, or until edges are brown. Cool cookies for 2 minutes on the baking sheets, and then transfer cookies to racks to cool completely.

5. While cookies bake, place raspberry jam in a saucepan over medium heat. Bring to a boil, stirring frequently, for 5 to 7 minutes, or until reduced by one-quarter. Spoon 1 teaspoon portions of jam into each cookie, and set allow jam to harden before storing cookies.

NOTE: Keep cookies in an airtight container, layered between sheets of waxed paper or parchment, at room temperature for up to 5 days.

✻ ACAPULCO GOLD POLVARONES (MEXICAN WEDDING COOKIES)

These rich and buttery cookies are a Tex-Mex version of shortbread. In Mexico they were made with lard, but I prefer the flavor given them by butter, especially "enhanced" butter.

YIELD: 3 dozen
ACTIVE TIME: 15 minutes
START TO FINISH: 30 minutes

1 cup (16 tablespoons) Bong Butter (page 23), softened
1¾ cups confectioners' sugar, divided
1 cup cake flour
1 cup self-rising flour
1 cup blanched almonds, very finely chopped
½ teaspoon pure vanilla extract, preferably Mexican

1. Preheat the oven to 350°F, and grease two baking sheets or line them with silicon baking mats.

2. Place butter in a mixing bowl with 1¼ cups sugar, and beat well at medium speed with an electric mixer until light and fluffy. Add cake flour, self-rising flour, almonds, and vanilla to the bowl, and mix briefly until just combined. The dough will be very stiff; add a few drops of hot water, if necessary, to make it pliable.

3. Take 1 tablespoon bits of dough, and roll it into a ball. Place balls 1 inch apart on the prepared baking sheets, and flatten balls slightly with the bottom of glass dipped in flour. Bake cookies for 12 to 15 minutes, or until lightly browned. Remove cookies from the oven.

4. Sift remaining ½ cup sugar into a low bowl, and transfer cookies a few at a time to the bowl with a spatula. Coat cookies with sugar, and then transfer cookies to racks to cool completely.

NOTE: Keep cookies in an airtight container, layered between sheets of waxed paper or parchment, at room temperature for up to 5 days. Cookies can also be frozen for up to 2 months.

VARIATION:

• Substitute pecans, toasted in a 350°F oven for 5 to 7 minutes, for the almonds.

Part of the plum family, the almond tree is native
to North Africa, West Asia, and the Mediterranean.
The English word almond is derived from the French
amande, which in turn is a derivative of the old Latin word
for almond, amygdalus, literally meaning "tonsil plum."

✿ AUNT MARY'S TROPICAL DRIED FRUIT AND NUT COOKIES

There's a whole lot going on in these chewy cookies with different nuts and fruits all mixed together in that special buttery base. They're similar to a fruitcake but ever so much better.

YIELD: 5 to 6 dozen
ACTIVE TIME: 20 minutes
START TO FINISH: 35 minutes

½ pound raw cashew nuts
½ pound blanched almonds
½ pound pitted dates, chopped
½ pound dried figs, stemmed and chopped
½ pound candied pineapple, chopped
2½ cups all-purpose flour, divided
1 cup (16 tablespoons) Bong Butter (page 23), softened

1 cup granulated sugar
½ cup firmly packed light brown sugar
2 large eggs
1 teaspoon rum extract
1 teaspoon baking soda
1 teaspoon ground cinnamon
½ teaspoon salt

1. Preheat the oven to 350°F. Line two baking sheets with parchment paper or silicon baking mats. Place cashews and almonds on a baking sheet, and toast for 5 to 7 minutes, or until lightly browned. Remove the pan from the oven, and coarsely chop nuts in a food processor fitted with a steel blade, using on-and-off pulsing, or by hand. Increase oven temperature to 375°F.

2. Combine cashews, almonds, dates, figs, and candied pineapple in a mixing bowl. Toss with ½ cup of the flour, and mix well so that the pieces separate.

3. Combine butter, granulated sugar, and brown sugar in a large mixing bowl, and beat at low speed with an electric mixer to blend. Increase the speed to high, and beat for 3 to 4 minutes, or until light and fluffy. Add eggs, rum extract, baking soda, cinnamon, and salt, and beat for 2 minutes more. Reduce the speed to low and add remaining flour until just blended in. Stir in nut and dried fruit mixture.

4. Drop batter by tablespoons onto the baking sheets, spacing them 2 inches apart. Bake for 10 to 12 minutes or until edges are brown. Cool for 2 minutes on the baking sheets, and then transfer cookies to racks to cool completely.

NOTE: Keep cookies in an airtight container, layered between sheets of waxed paper or parchment, at room temperature for up to 5 days. Cookies can also be frozen for up to 2 months.

VARIATION:

• Substitute ground ginger for cinnamon, and add ¼ cup finely chopped crystallized ginger to the dough.

Cinnamon is the inner bark of a tropical evergreen tree that's harvested during the rainy season and then allowed to dry. At that time it's sold as sticks or ground. What we call cinnamon is cassia cinnamon, and there's also a Ceylon cinnamon that is less pungent.

✺ OATMEAL CRANBERRY CHRISTMAS BUD COOKIES

Just because it's a swap party doesn't mean that old favorites like oatmeal cookies shouldn't be included! Replacing raisins with tangy, colorful dried cranberries gives the cookies that Christmas touch.

YIELD: 3 to 4 dozen cookies
ACTIVE TIME: 15 minutes
START TO FINISH: 30 minutes

1 cup chopped walnuts
⅓ cup (6 tablespoons) Bong Butter (page 23), softened
½ cup granulated sugar
½ cup firmly packed dark brown sugar
2 large eggs, at room temperature
1 teaspoon pure vanilla extract

1 teaspoon ground cinnamon
½ teaspoon baking soda
Pinch of salt
1 cup all-purpose flour
1¼ cups quick-cooking or old-fashioned oats (not instant)
1 cup dried cranberries

1. Preheat the oven to 350°F, and grease two baking sheets or line them with silicon baking mats. Place walnuts on a baking sheet, and toast for 5 to 7 minutes, or until lightly browned. Increase oven temperature to 375°F.

2. Combine butter, granulated sugar, and brown sugar in a mixing bowl, and beat at low speed with an electric mixer to blend. Increase the speed to high, and beat for 3 to 4 minutes, or until light and fluffy. Add eggs, vanilla, cinnamon, baking soda, and salt, and beat for 2 minutes more. Reduce the speed to low and add flour until just blended in. Stir in oats, cranberries, and walnuts.

3. Drop batter by tablespoons onto the baking sheets, spacing them 2 inches apart. Bake for 12 to 15 minutes, or until edges are brown. Cool for 2 minutes on the baking sheets, and then transfer cookies to racks to cool completely.

NOTE: Keep cookies in an airtight container, layered between sheets of waxed paper or parchment, at room temperature for up to 5 days. Cookies can also be frozen for up to 2 months.

VARIATION:

• Substitute chopped dried apricots or raisins for the dried cranberries.

The cranberry, along with the blueberry and Concord grape, is one of North America's three native fruits that are still commercially grown. Native Americans, who discovered the wild berry's versatility as a food, fabric dye, and healing agent, first used cranberries.

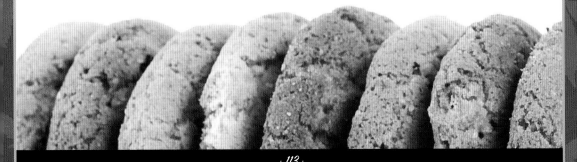

GANGA GRANOLA COOKIES

These are similar to oatmeal cookies but they're more complex in flavor and texture. There's coconut as well as oats, and then trail mix is in there too with all sorts of ingredients and flavors.

YIELD: 3 to 4 dozen
ACTIVE TIME: 15 minutes
START TO FINISH: 30 minutes

1 cup (16 tablespoons) Bong Butter (page 23), softened
1 cup firmly packed light brown sugar
¾ cup granulated sugar
2 large eggs
1 teaspoon pure vanilla extract
¾ cup all-purpose flour
½ cup whole wheat flour
1 teaspoon baking soda
½ teaspoon baking powder
½ teaspoon ground cinnamon
¼ teaspoon salt
2 cups old-fashioned oats
½ cup unsweetened flaked coconut
2 cups trail mix, coarsely chopped

1. Preheat the oven to 350°F, and grease two baking sheets or line them with silicon baking mats.

2. Combine butter, brown sugar, and granulated sugar in a mixing bowl, and beat at low speed with an electric mixer to blend. Increase the speed to high, and beat for 3 to 4 minutes, or until light and fluffy. Beat in eggs and vanilla. Beat in all-purpose flour, whole wheat flour, baking soda, baking powder, cinnamon, and salt at low speed. Stir in oats, coconut, and trail mix by hand.

3. Drop dough by tablespoons onto prepared baking sheets, 1½ inches apart. Bake cookies for 12 to 15 minutes, or until browned. Allow cookies to cool for 3 minutes on baking sheets, and then transfer cookies to racks to cool completely.

NOTE: Keep cookies in an airtight container, layered between sheets of waxed paper or parchment, at room temperature for up to 5 days. Cookies can also be frozen for up to 2 months.

VARIATION:

• Substitute ground ginger for the cinnamon and substitute granola cereal for the trail mix.

Willie Nelson is quoted as saying, "I think people need to be educated to the fact that marijuana is not a drug. Marijuana is an herb and a flower. God put it here. If He put it here and He wants it to grow, what gives the government the right to say that God is wrong?"

SPICY SWAG GINGER MAPLE COOKIES

These cookies are a lot easier to make than gingerbread people, and there's a surprise in the maple flavor complementing the ginger.

YIELD: 3 dozen
ACTIVE TIME: 20 minutes
START TO FINISH: 45 minutes

¾ cup (12 tablespoons) Bong Butter (page 23), softened
1 cup maple sugar
1 large egg, at room temperature
¼ cup pure maple syrup
½ cup finely chopped crystallized ginger
2 teaspoons baking soda
1 teaspoon ground ginger
¼ teaspoon salt
2½ cups all-purpose flour
½ cup granulated sugar

1. Preheat the oven to 350°F. Line two baking sheets with parchment paper or silicon baking mats.

2. Combine butter and maple sugar in a mixing bowl, and beat at low speed with an electric mixer to blend. Increase the speed to high, and beat for 3 to 4 minutes, or until light and fluffy. Beat in egg, maple syrup, crystallized ginger, baking soda, ground ginger, and salt and beat for 1 minute. Slowly add flour to the butter mixture, and beat until soft dough forms.

3. Roll dough in scant 1-tablespoon portions into balls, and roll balls in granulated sugar. Place balls 1½ inches apart on the baking sheets.

4. Bake cookies for 12 to 15 minutes, or until top surface is cracked. Cool cookies for 2 minutes on the baking sheets, and then transfer cookies to racks to cool completely.

NOTE: Keep cookies in an airtight container, layered between sheets of waxed paper or parchment, at room temperature for up to 5 days. Cookies can also be frozen for up to 2 months.

VARIATION:
• Substitute firmly packed light brown sugar for maple sugar, and substitute light molasses for maple syrup.

✻ ✻

Early New England settlers sweetened foods with maple syrup because white sugar had to be imported and was, therefore, expensive. Tapping the sugar maple trees native to North America and creating syrup from the sap is another skill the Native Americans taught the settlers

✻ ✻

❊ CRACKED UP CHOCOLATE ALMOND CRINKLE COOKIES

Powder-coated cookies—with the powder being confectioners' sugar, of course—are an important component of every swap party. These deliver great chocolate flavor, and the white coating makes them look like a slab of marble.

YIELD: 5 dozen
ACTIVE TIME: 25 minutes
START TO FINISH: 2¾ hours, including 2 hours to chill dough

⅔ cup slivered almonds

2 tablespoons granulated sugar

6 ounces bittersweet chocolate, finely chopped

¼ cup whole milk

½ cup (8 tablespoons) Bong Butter (page 23), softened

1½ cups packed light brown sugar

2 large eggs, at room temperature

½ teaspoon pure almond extract

2 tablespoons unsweetened cocoa powder

2 teaspoons baking powder

½ teaspoon salt

2¾ cups all-purpose flour

¾ cup confectioners' sugar

1. Preheat the oven to 350°F. Place almonds on a baking sheet, and toast for 5 to 7 minutes, or until lightly browned. Remove the pan from the oven, and combine nuts and granulated sugar in a food processor fitted with the steel blade. Chop very finely using on-and-off pulsing, or by hand. Set aside.

2. Combine chocolate and milk in a microwave-safe dish. Microwave on Medium (50 percent power) for 45 seconds. Stir, and repeat as necessary until chocolate mixture is melted and smooth. Set aside to cool.

3. Combine butter and brown sugar in a mixing bowl, and beat at low speed with an electric mixer to blend. Increase the speed to high, and beat for 3 to 4 minutes, or until light and fluffy. Beat in eggs, 1 at a time, and then beat in melted chocolate mixture, almond extract, cocoa, baking powder, and salt. Beat for 1 minute. Slowly add flour to butter mixture, and beat until stiff dough forms. Stir in almond mixture. Chill dough for at least 2 hours, or until firm.

4. Preheat the oven to 350°F. Line 2 baking sheets with parchment paper or silicon baking mats.

5. Sift confectioners' sugar onto a sheet of waxed paper. Roll 1-tablespoon portions of dough into balls, and then roll each in confectioners' sugar until well coated. Place balls 2 inches apart on baking sheets.

6. Bake cookies for 14 to 16 minutes, or until cookies are crackled and the edges feel dry. Cool cookies for 2 minutes on the baking sheets, and then transfer cookies to racks to cool completely.

NOTE: Keep cookies in an airtight container, layered between sheets of waxed paper or parchment, at room temperature for up to 5 days. Cookies can also be frozen for up to 2 months.

VARIATION:

• Substitute pecans for the almonds, and substitute pure vanilla extract for the almond extract.

Ancient Romans also referred to almonds as "Greek nuts," since they were first cultivated in Greece. Almonds date back in print to the Bible. A recipe from the Forme of Cury, dating back to 1390, uses blanched, ground almonds in a gravy for oysters

POWDER-COVERED MOCHA BASH BALLS

Whoever decided that chocolate and coffee should have a baby named mocha should get the Nobel Prize in chemistry. These two dark flavors are spectacular together, especially when a goodly amount of Bong Butter is added in.

YIELD: 3 dozen
ACTIVE TIME: 20 minutes
START TO FINISH: 45 minutes

2 tablespoons instant coffee
2 tablespoons boiling water
½ cup (8 tablespoons) Bong Butter (page 23), softened and cut into small pieces
⅓ cup granulated sugar
1 large egg, at room temperature
½ teaspoon pure vanilla extract
¼ cup unsweetened cocoa powder
1⅓ cups all-purpose flour
Pinch of salt
1 cup confectioners' sugar

1. Preheat the oven to 350°F, and grease two baking sheets or cover them with silicon baking mats. Combine coffee powder and water in a small bowl, and stir well to dissolve coffee. Set aside to cool.

2. Combine butter and sugar in a mixing bowl, and beat at medium speed with an electric mixer until light and fluffy. Add egg and vanilla, and beat well. Add cocoa powder and coffee mixture, and beat well, scraping the sides of the bowl as necessary. Reduce the speed to low, and add flour and salt. Beat until just combined.

3. Form dough into 1-inch balls, and place them 1 inch apart on the prepared baking sheets. Bake for 15 to 18 minutes, or until firm. Remove the pans from the oven.

4. Sift confectioners' sugar into a low bowl, and add a few cookies at a time, rolling them around in the sugar to coat them well. Transfer cookies to racks to cool completely.

NOTE: Keep cookies in an airtight container, layered between sheets of waxed paper or parchment, at room temperature for up to 5 days. Cookies can also be frozen for up to 2 months.

VARIATIONS:

- For coffee cookies, increase the instant coffee powder by 2 tablespoons and omit the cocoa.
- For chocolate cookies, omit the instant coffee, increase the cocoa powder to ⅓ cup, and add 2 tablespoons cold water to the dough.

✹ ✹

The best way to measure flour is by weighing it; that's the way professional pastry chefs do it. The reason is that how you treat the flour can influence the amount you get. The correct way is to spoon it from the bag into a measuring cup with a spoon, and then level it with a spatula, pushing the extra back into the bag. But what a lot of people do is level it by tapping the measuring cup on the counter. That compresses the flour and you get more than you think.

✹ ✹

❋ CHOCOLATE THAI SPICY CHIP COOKIES

Nothing like a jolt of black pepper to wake up your taste buds in this adult version of chocolate chip cookies! The sweet and spicy combo is outstanding when stoned.

YIELD: 3 dozen
ACTIVE TIME: 15 minutes
START TO FINISH: 45 minutes

1 cup (16 tablespoons) Bong Butter (page 23), softened
1 cup firmly packed light brown sugar
2 large eggs, at room temperature
1 teaspoon pure vanilla extract
1 teaspoon baking powder
1 teaspoon baking soda
1 teaspoon ground cinnamon
¼ teaspoon salt
⅛ teaspoon freshly ground black pepper
2 cups all-purpose flour
1 (12-ounce) bag bittersweet chocolate chips

1. Preheat the oven to 350°F. Line two baking sheets with parchment paper or silicon baking mats.

2. Combine butter and brown sugar in a mixing bowl, and beat at low speed with an electric mixer to blend. Increase the speed to high, and beat for 3 to 4 minutes, or until light and fluffy. Beat in eggs, vanilla, baking powder, baking soda, cinnamon, salt, and pepper, and beat for 1 minute. Slowly add flour to the butter mixture, and beat until soft dough forms. Stir in chocolate chips.

3. Drop batter by tablespoons onto the baking sheets, spacing them 2 inches apart. Bake for 10 to 12 minutes or until edges are brown. Cool for 2 minutes on the baking sheets, and then transfer cookies to racks to cool completely.

NOTE: Keep cookies in an airtight container, layered between sheets of waxed paper or parchment, at room temperature for up to 5 days. Cookies can also be frozen for up to 2 months.

VARIATION:
• Substitute butterscotch or white chocolate chips for the bittersweet chocolate.

Eggs should always be at room temperature when using them in baking, since the whites will not increase in volume properly if they are chilled. An easy way to do this is to place the eggs in a bowl of hot tap water for 5 minutes before separating them.

CHAPTER 6:

From Bon-Bons to Baklava: International Cookies or Cousins of Cookies

One aspect of a Pot Cookie Swap Party is that it's all adults. You don't have to worry about curtain climbers or rug rats handling cookies with sticky fingers. It also means that at least some of the concepts can be a bit more sophisticated than one-size-fits-all.

Christmas cookies in general are pretty homespun items, even if they have that extra glow from some ganga. But they're not universal. While almost all cultures have some sort of rolled sugar cookie, there are other forms tied to a specific country or region. Those are the sweet sensations you'll find in this chapter.

If people are bringing some truly ethnic cookies, ask them to decorate the platter with a flag from the country, and also ask them to add as much as they know about the history of the cookie to their recipe sheet.

SUGAR WEED SPRITZ

I always thought these cookies in fancy-dancy shapes were American. That shows you how little I knew about Christmas cookies before I starting working on this book! They're actually German, or they're Scandinavian, if you believe the Swedes. Wherever they were born, they're as much a part of Christmas as rolled sugar cookies, and they're a lot easier to make.

YIELD: 8 dozen
ACTIVE TIME: 25 minutes
START TO FINISH: 2 hours, including 1 hour to chill dough

1 cup (16 tablespoons) Bong Butter (page 23), softened
⅔ cup granulated sugar
2 large eggs, at room temperature
1 teaspoon pure vanilla extract
2½ cups all-purpose flour
¼ teaspoon salt
Colored coarse sugar crystals
Small candies
Candied cherries

1. Combine butter and sugar in a mixing bowl, and beat at low speed with an electric mixer to blend. Increase the speed to high, and beat for 3 to 4 minutes, or until light and fluffy. Beat in egg and vanilla, and beat for 1 minute. Slowly add flour and salt to the butter mixture, and beat until soft dough forms.

2. Divide dough in half, and wrap each half in plastic wrap. Press dough into a pancake. Refrigerate dough for 1 hour or until firm, or up to 2 days.

3. Preheat the oven to 350°F. Line two baking sheets with parchment paper or silicon baking mats.

4. Press dough through a cookie press onto the baking sheets, spacing them 1 inch apart. Decorate cookies with sugar crystals, candies, and candied cherries as desired.

5. Bake cookies for 12 to 15 minutes, or until edges are brown. Cool cookies for 2 minutes on the baking sheets, and then transfer them with a spatula to cooling racks to cool completely.

NOTE: Keep cookies in an airtight container, layered between sheets of waxed paper or parchment, at room temperature for up to 5 days. Cookies can also be frozen for up to 2 months.

VARIATIONS:

- Substitute almond extract for the vanilla extract, and substitute ½ cup almond meal for ½ cup of the flour.
- Substitute orange oil for the vanilla, and add 1 tablespoon grated orange zest to the dough.

If you don't have a cookie press, you can still make pretty cookies in interesting shapes. Pipe the dough through a pastry bag fitted with a star tip or a plain tip and pipe the dough into circles like a wreath. Then decorate and bake them.

LOCO WEED LINZER COOKIES

These cookies are hand-holdable versions of Austria's most famous dessert, the Linzertorte. It is believed to have originated in the city of Linz, and written recipes date back to the early eighteenth century. There's always some sort of nut as part of the pastry, and while in Austria it is filled with black currant preserves, in North America we usually use raspberry.

YIELD: 3 dozen
ACTIVE TIME: 35 minutes
START TO FINISH: 2 hours, including 1 hour to chill dough

¾ cup (12 tablespoons) Bong Butter (page 23), softened

1⅓ cups confectioners' sugar, divided

2 large eggs, at room temperature

2 teaspoons ground cinnamon

1 teaspoon baking powder

½ teaspoon freshly grated nutmeg

½ teaspoon salt

½ teaspoon pure vanilla extract

1¼ cups all-purpose flour

1¼ cups almond meal

½ cup raspberry jam

1. Combine butter and 1 cup sugar in a mixing bowl, and beat at low speed with an electric mixer to blend. Increase the speed to high, and beat for 3 to 4 minutes, or until light and fluffy. Beat in eggs, cinnamon, nutmeg, salt, and vanilla, and beat for 1 minute. Slowly add flour and almond meal to the butter mixture, and beat until soft dough forms.

2. Divide dough in half, and wrap each half in plastic wrap. Press dough into a pancake. Refrigerate dough for 1 hour or until firm, or up to 2 days.

3. Preheat oven to 325°F. Line two baking sheets with parchment paper or silicon baking mats.

4. Roll out half of dough on lightly floured surface to ⅛-inch thickness. Using a 2-inch round, scalloped edge cutter, cut out rounds. Using a ¾-inch star-shaped cutter, cut out center of half of rounds to make stars. Transfer all cookies to prepared sheets. Gather dough scraps; chill.

5. Bake cookies for 12 to 15 minutes, or until edges are brown. Cool cookies for 2 minutes on the baking sheets, and then transfer cookies to racks to cool completely.

6. Dust cookies with center hole with remaining confectioners' sugar. Place 1 teaspoon of raspberry jam on solid cookies, and form a sandwich with the two types of cookies.

NOTE: Keep cookies in an airtight container, layered between sheets of waxed paper or parchment, at room temperature for up to 5 days. Cookies can also be frozen for up to 2 months.

VARIATIONS:

• Substitute ground hazelnuts for the almond meal.
• Substitute blackberry or strawberry jam for the raspberry.

Did you know you could get a high from nutmeg? Probably not the tiny amount in these cookies or the sprinkle on a glass of eggnog at Christmas, but this spice has hallucinogenic properties. Who knew? The problem is that you usually get nauseous before you get high, so stick to stash. But if your cupboard is barren, there's always the spice pantry to explore.

RUSSIAN CHEERY CHERRY COOKIES

These happy little sugarcoated balls are similar in buttery richness to Acapulco Gold Polvarones (page 106), but instead of nuts they contain bits of sweet and bright candied cherries. Because the dough doesn't need time to chill they're quick to make too.

YIELD: 3 dozen
ACTIVE TIME: 20 minutes
START TO FINISH: 35 minutes

1 cup (16 tablespoons) Bong Butter (page 23), softened
1½ cups confectioners' sugar, divided
2 tablespoons kirsch, clear cherry brandy
½ teaspoon pure vanilla extract
2¼ cups all-purpose flour
¼ teaspoon salt
1 cup finely chopped candied cherries

1. Preheat the oven to 375°F. Line two baking sheets with parchment paper or silicon baking mats.

2. Combine butter and ½ cup sugar in a mixing bowl, and beat at low speed with an electric mixer to blend. Increase the speed to high, and beat for 3 to 4 minutes, or until light and fluffy. Beat in kirsch and vanilla, and beat for 1 minute.

Slowly add flour and salt to the butter mixture, and beat until soft dough forms. Fold cherries into dough.

3. Roll dough into 1-inch balls and arrange them 1 inch apart on baking sheets. Bake for 8 to 10 minutes, or until set and beginning to brown. Remove cookies from the oven.

4. Sift remaining sugar into a low bowl, and transfer cookies a few at a time to the bowl with a spatula. Coat cookies with sugar, and return them to the baking sheets. Bake for an additional 3 to 4 minutes, then remove them from the oven and coat then again with sugar. Transfer cookies to racks to cool completely.

NOTE: Keep cookies in an airtight container, layered between sheets of waxed paper or parchment, at room temperature for up to 5 days. Cookies can also be frozen for up to 2 months.

VARIATION:

• Substitute candied pineapple for the candied cherries, and substitute rum extract for the vanilla.

In Western culture, both in Europe and in the New World, cannabis was a footnote rather than a main topic. The Greek historian Herodotus writes of how the nomadic Scythian tribe, who lived in what we now call parts of Iran and to the Russian steppes as well as along the north side of the Black Sea, would burn the seeds as part of funeral rites. "The smell of it made them drunk, just as wine does us," was his commentary. It appears that no one was bitching at those Scythians' funerals about the evils of secondhand smoke.

✿ OLDE ENGLISH REVVED-UP RUM FRUITCAKE COOKIES

Unlike fruit cake, of which only one was ever made about a century ago and keeps being passed around the world, cookies made with some dried fruits, booze, and spices can be really great nibbles. That's what you'll think after eating some of this English recipe. Sure beats spotted dick too!

YIELD: 5 dozen
ACTIVE TIME: 25 minutes
START TO FINISH: 3½ hours, including 2 hours to macerate fruit

1 cup golden raisins
½ cup chopped candied cherries
½ cup dried currants (about 5 ounces)
½ cup chopped pitted dates
½ cup candied citrus peel
½ cup rum, treated as Booze with Buzz (page 26), divided
½ cup chopped walnuts
½ cup (8 tablespoons) Bong Butter (page 23), softened, divided
½ cup firmly packed light brown sugar
1 large egg, at room temperature
½ teaspoon rum extract

½ teaspoon baking powder
½ teaspoon apple pie spice
¼ teaspoon salt
1 cup all-purpose flour
1 cup confectioner's sugar
5 dozen 1-inch baking cups

1. Combine raisins, cherries, currants, dates, citrus peel, and ⅓ cup rum in a mixing bowl, and toss well. Allow mixture to sit for a minimum of 2 hours, and up to 24 hours at room temperature, covered with plastic wrap.

2. Preheat the oven to 350°F. Place walnuts on a baking sheet, and toast for 5 to 7 minutes, or until lightly browned. Reduce the oven temperature to 325°F.

3. Combine 5 tablespoons butter and sugar in a mixing bowl, and beat at low speed with an electric mixer to blend. Increase the speed to high, and beat for 3 to 4 minutes, or until light and fluffy. Beat in egg, rum extract, baking powder, apple pie spice, and salt, and beat for 1 minute. Slowly add flour to butter mixture, and beat to combine. Fold dried fruit mixture and walnuts into dough.

4. Drop heaping teaspoons of dough into 1-inch paper baking cups. Bake for 20 to 24 minutes, or until lightly brown. Transfer cups to a cooling rack, and cool completely.

5. Combine remaining butter, confectioners' sugar, and remaining rum in a mixing bowl, and beat at low speed with an electric mixer to blend. Increase the speed to high, and beat for 2 to 3 minutes, or until light and fluffy. Spread frosting on cooled cookies.

NOTE: Keep cookies in an airtight container, layered between sheets of waxed paper or parchment, at room temperature for up to 5 days.

Brown sugar is granulated sugar mixed with molasses, and the darker the color, the more pronounced the molasses flavor. If a recipe calls for dark brown sugar, and you only have light brown sugar, add 2 tablespoons molasses per ½ cup sugar to replicate the taste.

⚕ LATIN AMERICAN COCONUT PEANUT COOKIES (GALLETAS MARIA)

This is a great cookie to suggest to someone coming to your swap party who doesn't own an electric mixer because it doesn't require one. The rich dough—containing oats, coconut, and peanuts—starts on the stove.

YIELD: 3 dozen
ACTIVE TIME: 20 minutes
START TO FINISH: 1 hour, including 30 minutes to rest dough

¾ cup (12 tablespoons) Bong Butter (page 23), softened
¾ cup firmly packed light brown sugar
1 large egg, at room temperature
1 teaspoon baking powder
½ teaspoon ground cinnamon
¼ teaspoon baking soda
¼ teaspoon salt
1½ cups all-purpose flour
1 cup shredded sweetened coconut
¾ cup rolled oats
¾ cup chopped roasted peanuts

1. Melt butter in a saucepan over medium heat. Stir in sugar, and cook over low heat until sugar mixture is saucy. Whisk in egg, baking powder, cinnamon, baking soda, and salt. Stir in flour, and then fold in coconut, oats, and peanuts. Set aside for 30 minutes, or until mixture reaches room temperature and thickens.

2. Preheat the oven to 400°F. Line two baking sheets with parchment paper or silicon baking mats.

3. Drop batter by tablespoons onto the baking sheets, spacing them 2 inches apart. Bake for 10 to 12 minutes or until edges are brown. Cool for 2 minutes on the baking sheets, and then transfer cookies to racks to cool completely.

NOTE: Keep cookies in an airtight container, layered between sheets of waxed paper or parchment, at room temperature for up to 5 days. Cookies can also be frozen for up to 2 months.

＊＊＊＊＊＊＊＊＊＊＊＊＊＊＊＊＊＊＊＊＊＊＊＊＊＊＊＊＊＊＊＊＊＊＊＊

We all know how creative we feel when we're stoned, and a bunch of creative Bohemian types in Paris actually celebrated weed. Called the Club de Hashischins, it was active from 1844 to 1849 in Paris, with a hangout in the Hotel de Lauzun on the Ile St. Louis. The members of the Club were the intellectual elite of the day including painter Eugene Delacroix and writers Alexandre Dumas, Theophile Gautier, and Charles Baudelaire. One member of the group was a noted psychiatrist of the day, Dr. Jacques-Joseph Moreau. He was the first to publish work on the effect of drugs on the central nervous system.

＊＊＊＊＊＊＊＊＊＊＊＊＊＊＊＊＊＊＊＊＊＊＊＊＊＊＊＊＊＊＊＊＊＊＊＊

BONGED UP BAKLAVA

When it comes to gooey goodness, there's nothing that beats classic Greek baklava in my opinion. Crispy layers of thin phyllo are just soaked in loaded butter, and then topped with a lemony sugar syrup.

YIELD: 4 dozen (2-inch) pieces
ACTIVE TIME: 40 minutes
START TO FINISH: 1½ hours

3½ cups walnuts
2½ cups granulated sugar, divided
1 teaspoon ground cinnamon
¼ teaspoon ground cloves
1 (1 pound) package phyllo sheets, thawed

1½ cups (24 tablespoons) Bong Butter (page 23), melted
1½ cups water
½ cup honey
½ lemon, thinly sliced
1 (3-inch) cinnamon stick

1. Preheat the oven to 350°F. Place walnuts on a baking sheet, and toast for 5 to 7 minutes, or until lightly browned. Remove the pan from the oven, and combine nuts, ½ cup sugar, cinnamon, and cloves in a food processor fitted with the steel blade. Chop very finely using on-and-off pulsing or by hand.

2. Increase the oven temperature to 375°F, and grease a 12 x 16-inch rimmed baking sheet pan. Place phyllo on a plate, and cover it with plastic wrap or a damp paper towel to keep it from drying out.

3. Place 1 sheet of phyllo in the baking pan, and brush with melted butter. Repeat with 7 other sheets, and sprinkle with ⅓ of nut mixture. Place 4 more sheets of phyllo on top of nut mixture, brushing each with butter. Sprinkle with ⅓ of nut mixture, and then repeat. Top last round of nut mixture with remaining sheets of phyllo, brushing each, including the top one, with butter. Trim edges to make a neat rectangle.

4. Cut pastry into 2-inch squares or triangles through the 3 nut layers. Do not cut through the bottom crust. Bake for 25 to 30 minutes, or until the top layer of phyllo is brown.

5. Prepare syrup while pastry bakes. Combine remaining 2 cups sugar, water, honey, lemon, and cinnamon stick in a saucepan. Bring to a boil over medium heat, stirring occasionally. Reduce the heat to low, and simmer syrup for 5 minutes. Strain syrup, and keep hot.

6. Remove the pan from the oven and immediately pour hot syrup over the baklava. Place pan on a cooling rack, and cool to room temperature. Cut through bottom layer of crust once cooled.

NOTE: Keep baklava in an airtight container, layered between sheets of waxed paper or parchment, at room temperature for up to 5 days.

VARIATION:
• Substitute pecans, macadamia nuts, or almonds for the walnuts.

Pastry brushes are expensive, but paintbrushes are cheap.
Any natural-bristle paintbrush can be used
as a pastry brush. But don't use one of those
foam rubber brushes because the foam is
not approved for human consumption.
It's got chemicals in it.

✿ WARSAW WOWIE FRIED COOKIES (CHRUSTI)

These crispy Polish cookies are like tiny doughnuts, only with a richer flavor. Once dusted with confectioners' sugar, they're like miniature snowflakes playing on your tongue.

YIELD: 4 dozen
ACTIVE TIME: 20 minutes
START TO FINISH: 1 1/2 hours

3 large eggs, at room temperature
1/4 cup whole milk
3/4 cup granulated sugar
1/2 cup (8 tablespoons) Bong Butter (page 23), melted
1 teaspoon baking soda
1 teaspoon pure vanilla extract
1/2 teaspoon salt
1/2 teaspoon freshly ground nutmeg
3 1/2 cups all-purpose flour, plus additional for rolling
Vegetable oil for frying
1 cup confectioners' sugar for dusting

1. Combine eggs, milk, granulated sugar, and butter in a mixing bowl, and whisk well. Whisk in baking soda, vanilla, salt, and nutmeg. Add flour, and mix well until it forms a soft dough. Refrigerate dough, tightly covered, for at least 1 hour, or up to 3 days.

2. Dust a counter and rolling pin with flour. Roll out dough to an even thickness of ¼ inch. Cut dough into strips 1 inch wide. Cut strips on a diagonal at 3-inch intervals to form diamond shapes.

3. Pour oil to a depth of 1½ inches in a deep-sided saucepan. Heat oil to a temperature of 375°F on a candy/deep fry thermometer. Add a few cookies at a time to the pan, turning cookies with a slotted spoon to brown on both sides.

4. Drain cookies on paper towels, and sift confectioners' sugar on them. Serve immediately.

NOTE: The cookies can be fried up to 2 days in advance and kept in an airtight container at room temperature. Do not dust with sugar if storing. Reheat the cookies in a 250°F oven for 3 to 5 minutes, then dust with sugar and serve.

VARIATION:

• Substitute orange oil for the vanilla extract, and add 1 tablespoon grated orange zest to the dough.

Confectioners' sugar contains a small amount of cornstarch, which acts as a binding agent. If you make whipped cream with confectioners' sugar it will not separate as easily as cream beaten with granulated sugar.

sugar

GANGA GANACHE FRENCH CHOCOLATE BON-BONS

The batter for this luscious chocolate cake is created in a matter of minutes in a food processor. It's a dense and rich cake that is crunchy with nuts and topped with a candy-like ganache.

YIELD: 16 bon-bons
ACTIVE TIME: 15 minutes
START TO FINISH: 1½ hours, including 1 hour for chilling

10 ounces bittersweet chocolate, chopped, divided
2 cups pecan or walnut halves, toasted in a 350°F oven for 5 minutes
1 cup (16 tablespoons) Bong Butter (page 23), softened, divided
2 tablespoons plus ½ cup granulated sugar
3 large eggs, at room temperature
1 tablespoon rum, treated according to the formulation for Booze with Buzz (page 26)

1. Preheat the oven to 375°F. Grease an 8 x 8-inch pan, cut out a square of waxed paper or parchment to fit the bottom, and grease the paper.

2. Melt 4 ounces chocolate in a microwave oven or over simmering water in a double boiler. Cool slightly. Chop nuts with 2 tablespoons sugar in a food processor fitted with a steel blade, using on-and-off pulsing. Scrape nuts into a bowl.

3. Scrape batter into the prepared pan and bake for 25 minutes. The cake will be soft but will firm up as it cools. Remove cake from the oven and cool 20 minutes on a cooling rack. Invert cake onto a plate, remove the paper, and cool completely. Cut cake into 2-inch squares.

4. To make glaze, combine remaining 6 ounces chocolate and remaining 8 tablespoons butter in a small saucepan. Melt over low heat and beat until shiny and smooth. Place cake cubes on a rack over a sheet of wax paper. Spoon glaze over the squares, and allow to sit in a cool place until chocolate hardens.

NOTE: The squares can be prepared 2 days in advance and refrigerated. Allow them to reach room temperature before serving.

VARIATIONS:
- Add 1 tablespoon instant espresso powder to the batter.
- Substitute Triple Sec or Grand Marnier for the rum, and add 2 teaspoons grated orange zest to the batter.
- Substitute blanched almonds for the pecans or walnuts, substitute amaretto for the rum, and add ½ teaspoon pure almond extract to the batter.

CHAPTER 7

· ·

Stove-Top Sensations: Candy and Confections

If you've got a bunch of bar cookies from Chapter 4 in the oven, they're going to take considerable time to cook. So you think "hmmm... what can I make that doesn't need an oven?" That's when the recipes in this chapter enter the picture. You can whip up a batch in less time than the cookies take to bake, and you've got another treat ready to enjoy at the swap party.

A lot of cookie swaps around the country don't allow candy and other confections because they're not really cookies. But most cookie swaps aren't based around the concept of chewing your cheeba, and we all know how intensely flavored candies are. That intense sweetness is just accentuated when you're stoned.

The best way to present the recipes in this chapter at your swap party is in those cute little paper cups. They're about an inch in diameter, and hold cubes and balls well. There are a few recipes that make irregular shapes, and they can be packaged in cupcake holders (also paper and also cute).

🍁 Sugar Stages

We've got to get serious for a minute to make sure your candies are as yummy as your cookies. Most candy recipes instruct you to boil your sugar mixture until it reaches a certain temperature. The final texture of candy depends on the sugar concentration. As the syrup is heated, it boils, water evaporates, the sugar concentration increases, and the boiling point rises. A given temperature corresponds to a particular sugar concentration. In general, higher temperatures and greater sugar concentrations result in hard, brittle candies, and lower temperatures result in softer candies.

For the best results and most accuracy, use a candy thermometer. However, if you don't have one there is a classic test conducted by dropping a few droplets of the boiling syrup into ice water and then feeling the result. If you want to practice what this means, bring some sugar syrup to a boil, and then test it every few minutes to feel the result. Here are the stages of sugar:

- Thread stage: 230 to 233°F, with sugar concentration at 80 percent. This is used for the sorts of syrup you'd use on ice cream. At this temperature the liquid forms threads but does not form a ball.

- Soft ball stage: 234 to 240°F, with sugar concentration at 85 percent. This is the temperature used for fudge and other soft candies. Sugar syrup dropped into cold water will form a soft, flexible ball. If you remove the ball from water, it will flatten like a pancake after a few moments in your hand.

- Firm ball stage: 244 to 248°F, with sugar concentration at 87 percent. This is the temperature used for caramel candies and other candies with medium density. Drop a little of this syrup in cold water and it will form a firm ball, one that won't flatten when you take it out of the water, but remains malleable and will flatten when squeezed.

- Hard ball stage: 250 to 266°F, with sugar concentration at 92 percent. This is the temperature for nougat and other chewy and dense candy. A little of this syrup dropped into cold water will form a hard ball. If you take the ball out of the water, it won't flatten. The ball will be hard, but you can still change its shape by squashing it.

- Soft crack stage: 270 to 290°F, with sugar concentration at 95 percent. Saltwater taffy is made with sugar at this temperature. As the syrup reached soft-crack stage, the bubbles on top will become smaller, thicker, and closer together. At this stage, the moisture content is low. When you drop a bit of this syrup into cold water, it will solidify into threads that, when removed from the water, are flexible, not brittle. They will bend slightly before breaking.

- Hard crack stage: 295 to 310°F with a sugar concentration of 99 percent. This temperature is needed for brittles and butter toffee. The hard-crack stage is the highest temperature you are likely to see specified in a candy recipe. At these temperatures, there is almost no water left in the syrup. Drop a little of the molten syrup in cold water and it will form hard, brittle threads that break when bent.

• Caramelized sugar: 320 to 340°F, with a sugar concentration of 100 percent. The lower end of this range the liquid is clear, and as it climbs in temperature it turns to a golden and then deeper brown. This is what is used to make caramel sauce, not caramel candies.

The temperatures specified here are for sea level. At higher altitudes, subtract 1°F from every listed temperature for each 500 feet above sea level.

As you can see, a few degrees in one direction or another can change the results of the candy, so it's a good idea to test your thermometer's accuracy by placing it in plain boiling water. At sea level, it should read 212°F. If it reads above or below this number, make the necessary adjustments when cooking your sugar syrup.

☘ ACAPULCO GOLD MEXICAN BROWN SUGAR FUDGE

This Mexican butterscotch fudge is the epitome of what you're craving as sweet munchies. And its combo of "leaded" ingredients keeps the high movin' right along.

YIELD: 5 dozen
ACTIVE TIME: 30 minutes
START TO FINISH: 1 hour, including 30 minutes to chill

⅔ cup Bhang Booster (page 25)
2 cups firmly packed light brown sugar
¾ cup (12 tablespoons) Bong Butter (page 23), sliced
Pinch of salt
1 teaspoon pure vanilla extract, preferably Mexican
1½ cups confectioners' sugar
1 cup roasted peanuts
Vegetable oil spray

1. Line a 9 x 9-inch pan with aluminum foil, allowing it to extend at least 3 inches over the sides. Spray the foil with vegetable oil spray.

2. Combine Bhang Booster, brown sugar, butter, salt, and vanilla in a saucepan, and bring to a boil over medium heat, stirring to dissolve sugar.

3. Reduce the heat to medium-low, and simmer mixture for 15 to 20 minutes or until it looks thicker and syrupy.

4. Remove the pan from the heat, and beat in the confectioners' sugar with an electric mixer at low speed. Beat for 3 to 5 minutes, or until mixture is thick and smooth. Stir in peanuts, and scrape fudge into the pan, and refrigerate for 30 minutes, or until firm.

5. Lift fudge from the pan with the foil, and cut into squares.

NOTE: The squares can be stored refrigerated for up to 1 week. Place them in an airtight container with sheets of plastic wrap in between the layers.

VARIATIONS:

- Add ¾ cup chopped roasted peanuts to fudge, or sprinkle them on top of fudge before chilling.
- Add 1 teaspoon ground cinnamon to fudge for a spicier flavor.

The only difference between butterscotch and caramel is that butterscotch starts with brown sugar rather than white sugar. Most Mexican and Latin American recipes use light brown sugar because it's the closest to the region's unrefined sugar.

☘ SWEET LUCY'S SOUTHERN PECAN PRALINES

Pralines are part of the tradition of Southern sweets, and these are incredibly easy to make. The cream and butter balance the sweetness with richness.

YIELD: 3 dozen
ACTIVE TIME: 25 minutes
START TO FINISH: 1 hour

3 cups pecan halves
3 cups firmly packed light brown sugar
1 cup heavy cream
½ teaspoon cream of tartar
½ teaspoon salt
6 tablespoons Bong Butter (page 23), thinly sliced
¾ teaspoon pure vanilla extract
Vegetable oil spray

1. Preheat the oven to 350°F. Place pecans on a baking sheet, and toast for 5 to 7 minutes, or until lightly browned. Spray two baking sheets with vegetable oil spray.

2. Combine brown sugar, cream, cream of tartar, and salt in a saucepan. Place the pan over medium heat, and swirl the pan by its handle until sugar dissolves. Raise the heat to medium-high, and continue to cook, stirring constantly, for 15 to 18 minutes, or until mixture registers 236°F on a candy thermometer, the soft ball stage.

3. Stir in butter and vanilla, and cool mixture to a temperature of 220°F. Beat at medium speed with an electric mixer for 2 minutes, or until mixture is creamy. Stir in pecans.

4. Drop mixture by 1-tablespoon portions onto the prepared baking sheets. Let pralines harden at room temperature.

NOTE: The pralines can be stored at room temperature for up to 1 week. Place them in an airtight container with sheets of waxed paper in between the layers.

VARIATION:
• For New England Pralines, substitute walnut halves for the pecans, and substitute maple sugar for the light brown sugar.

✱✱✱✱✱✱✱✱✱✱✱✱✱✱✱✱✱✱✱✱✱✱✱✱✱✱✱✱✱✱✱✱✱✱✱✱✱✱

It is widely agreed that pralines are named after a French diplomat from the early seventeenth century whose name and title was César, duc de Choiseul, comte du Plessis-Praslin. The actual creator of the praline is believed to be his personal chef, Clement Lassagne, but there are many versions of the story.

✱✱✱✱✱✱✱✱✱✱✱✱✱✱✱✱✱✱✱✱✱✱✱✱✱✱✱✱✱✱✱✱✱✱✱✱✱✱

SUGAR WEED SPICED PEANUT BRITTLE

The addition of some aromatic spices from Chinese five-spice powder adds interest to the sweet and crunchy morsels of this typical Southern sweet.

YIELD: 3 to 4 dozen
ACTIVE TIME: 25 minutes
START TO FINISH: 1 hour

1 cup (16 tablespoons) Bong Butter (page 23), sliced
1 cup granulated sugar
2 tablespoons water
2 tablespoons light corn syrup
1 teaspoon Chinese five-spice powder
¼ teaspoon salt
1½ cups roasted peanuts (not dry-roasted)
Vegetable oil spray

1. Prepare a lipped baking sheet by lining it with heavy-duty aluminum foil and spraying the foil with vegetable oil spray. Set aside.

2. Melt butter in a medium saucepan over medium heat. Stir in sugar, water, and corn syrup, and mix well. Cook mixture over medium heat, stirring frequently, until it registers 290°F on a candy thermometer, the soft crack stage. Stir in Chinese five-spice powder, salt, and peanuts.

3. Pour mixture immediately onto the prepared baking sheet. Tilt the sheet several times to spread candy in a thin layer. Allow brittle to sit at room temperature until it is completely cool. Break brittle into small pieces.

NOTE: The brittle can be stored at room temperature for up to 1 week. Place pieces in an airtight container with sheets of waxed paper in between the layers.

VARIATIONS:
- Substitute any nut for the peanuts. If the nuts are raw, toast them in a 350°F oven for 5 to 7 minutes, or until browned.
- Substitute cinnamon or apple pie spice for the Chinese five-spice powder.

The first notable increase in peanut consumption in the United States was in 1860 with the outbreak of the Civil War. Soldiers on both sides turned to peanuts for food. They took their taste for peanuts home with them and peanuts were sold freshly roasted by street vendors and at baseball games and circuses.

KENTUCKY BLUE BOURBON BALLS

It doesn't get much easier than these candies to make, and you've got a double buzz because the bourbon is infused with weed. Confectioners' sugar and butter candies are part of Christmas, and these will make a great addition to your swap.

YIELD: 3 to 4 dozen
ACTIVE TIME: 25 minutes
START TO FINISH: 3½ hours, including 2¾ hours to chill

2 cups chopped pecans
1 cup (16 tablespoons) Bong Butter (page 23), softened
2 pounds confectioners' sugar
½ cup bourbon treated as Booze with Buzz (page 26)
½ teaspoon salt
½ pound bittersweet chocolate

1. Preheat the oven to 350°F. Place pecans on a baking sheet, and toast for 5 to 7 minutes, or until lightly browned. Remove nuts from the oven, and set aside.

2. Combine butter and 1 pound confectioners' sugar in a mixing bowl, and beat at low speed with an electric mixer to blend. Increase the speed to high, and beat for 3 to 4 minutes, or until light and fluffy. Add remaining sugar, bourbon, and salt, and beat for 2 minutes. Stir in pecans, and refrigerate the mixture for 2 hours, or until firm.

3. Break chocolate into pieces no larger than a lima bean. Either chop chocolate in a food processor fitted with a steel blade using on-and-off pulsing or place it in a heavy resealable plastic bag and smash it with the back of a heavy skillet. Melt chocolate according to one of the methods given on page 33. Cool chocolate to 105°F.

4. Cover a baking sheet with parchment paper or waxed paper. Form bourbon mixture into balls by scant tablespoons and arrange them on the baking sheet. Drizzle chocolate over balls. Refrigerate uncovered for 45 minutes, or until chocolate hardens. Then transfer balls to an airtight container.

NOTE: The balls can be stored refrigerated for up to 1 week. Place them in an airtight container with sheets of plastic wrap in between the layers.

VARIATIONS:

- Substitute rum for the bourbon and substitute macadamia nuts for the pecans.
- Substitute Grand Marnier for the bourbon, and add 1 tablespoon grated orange zest to the dough.

The French assisted in the Revolutionary War, and to thank them French names were given to new settlements or counties. In the Western part of Virginia, the then county of Kentucky was subdivided in 1780 and again in 1786. One of these subdivisions was named Bourbon County, after the French Royal House. That's why this truly American whiskey has a French name.

DOUBLE DOSE CHOCOLATE TRUFFLES

These are truffles for people who don't like candies too sweet. The addition of the unsweetened cocoa powder to the mix brings down the sugar level and increases the intense chocolate flavor.

YIELD: 2¹/₂ dozen
ACTIVE TIME: 20 minutes
START TO FINISH: 4½ hours, including 4 hours to chill

½ pound good-quality bittersweet chocolate
½ cup Bhang Booster (page 25)
½ cup (8 tablespoons) Bong Butter (page 23), sliced
Pinch of salt
²/₃ cup unsweetened cocoa powder, divided

1. Break chocolate into pieces no larger than a lima bean. Either chop chocolate in a food processor fitted with a steel blade using on-and-off pulsing or place it in a heavy resealable plastic bag and smash it with the back of a heavy skillet.

2. Heat Bhang Booster and butter in a saucepan over medium heat, stirring frequently, until mixture comes to a simmer. Stir in salt, and add chocolate and ¼ cup cocoa. Remove the pan from the heat, cover the pan, and allow chocolate to melt for 5 minutes. Whisk mixture until smooth, and transfer to a 9 x 9-inch baking pan. Chill mixture for at least 4 hours or overnight.

3. Place remaining cocoa powder in a shallow bowl. Using the large side of a melon baller, scoop out 2 teaspoons mixture, and gently form it into a ball. Roll balls in cocoa and then refrigerate for 30 minutes to set cocoa.

NOTE: The truffles can be made up to 1 week in advance and refrigerated, tightly covered with plastic wrap or in an airtight container. Allow them to sit at room temperature for 1 hour before serving.

VARIATIONS:
- Substitute milk chocolate for the bittersweet chocolate.
- Add ½ cup chopped toasted nuts to the truffle mixture.

✱✱

Cocoa powder has a tendency to become lumpy if exposed to humidity, and if you find that this is the case with your container, sift the cocoa or shake it through a fine-meshed sieve before using it. Those little lumps are difficult to remove otherwise.

✱✱

✿ MAUI WOWIE COCONUT CHOCOLATE FUDGE

Chocolate and coconut is one of my favorite combinations, and if you like it in a candy bar you'll love it in this fudge. It's creamy and intensely flavored; you'll go bonkers for it even before you go bonkers.

YIELD: 4 dozen
ACTIVE TIME: 10 minutes
START TO FINISH: 1¼ hours, including 1 hour to chill

6 (2-ounce) chocolate-covered coconut candy bars
2 cups granulated sugar
¾ cup (12 tablespoons) Bong Butter (page 23)
¾ cup Bhang Booster (page 25)
2 cups semisweet chocolate chips
1 (7-ounce) jar marshmallow cream
1 teaspoon coconut extract
Vegetable oil spray

1. Line a 9 x 9-inch pan with aluminum foil, allowing it to extend at least 3 inches over the sides. Spray the foil with vegetable oil spray. Cut candy bars into ½-inch slices, and set aside.

2. Combine sugar, butter, and Bhang Booster in a saucepan. Bring to a boil over medium heat, stirring occasionally. Cook, stirring frequently, for 3 to 4 minutes, or until mixture reaches 234°F (soft ball stage) on a candy thermometer.

3. Remove the pan from the heat, and stir in chocolate chips, marshmallow cream, and coconut extract.

4. Pour half of mixture into the pan, and top with half of candy slices. Repeat with remaining chocolate and candy slices.

5. Chill for 1 hour, or until set. Lift fudge out of the pan using the foil, and cut into squares.

NOTE: The fudge can be refrigerated for up to 1 week, tightly covered.

VARIATION:
- Substitute almond extract for the coconut extract, and add ¾ cup chopped almonds to the fudge mixture.

Think tropics and then think coconut. The name first appeared in English in the mid-sixteenth century; it comes from the Spanish and Portuguese word coco, which means "monkey face." The earlier explorers thought the three round markings at the base of the coconut looked like eyes and a mouth. In addition to being a food, also prized for its water, coconuts were the currency of the Nicobar Islands of the Indian Ocean until the early part of the twentieth century.

CHEEBA CHOCOLATE WALNUT FUDGE

This recipe is Nirvana for all of us who are admitted chocoholics! There's depth from unsweetened chocolate and intensity from bittersweet—plus the crunch of nuts.

YIELD: 6 dozen
ACTIVE TIME: 25 minutes
START TO FINISH: 1¾ hours, including 1 hour to chill

1 cup coarsely chopped walnuts
¾ pound (12 ounces) good-quality bittersweet chocolate
2 ounces unsweetened chocolate
½ cup (8 tablespoons) Bong Butter (page 23), sliced
2 cups granulated sugar
1 cup Bhang Booster (page 25)
1 teaspoon pure vanilla extract
Vegetable oil spray

1. Preheat the oven to 350°F. Line a 9 x 9-inch baking pan with heavy-duty aluminum foil, allowing it to extend over the top of the sides. Spray the foil with vegetable oil spray.

2. Place walnuts on a baking sheet, and toast for 5 to 7 minutes, or until lightly browned. Remove nuts from the oven, and set aside.

3. Break bittersweet chocolate and unsweetened chocolate into pieces no larger than a lima bean. Either chop chocolate in a food processor fitted with a steel blade using on-and-off pulsing or place it in a heavy resealable plastic bag and smash it with the back of a heavy skillet. Place chocolate and butter in a mixing bowl, and set aside.

4. Combine sugar and Bhang Booster in a deep saucepan, and cook over medium heat until sugar dissolves and mixture comes to boil. Continue to cook, stirring constantly, for 15 to 18 minutes, or until mixture registers 236°F (soft ball stage) on a candy thermometer.

5. Pour hot mixture over chocolate and butter, and whisk until smooth. Stir in walnuts and vanilla.

6. Spread fudge evenly in the prepared pan. Refrigerate, uncovered, for 1 to 2 hours, or until cold and set. Lift fudge from the pan with the foil, and cut into squares.

NOTE: The squares can be stored refrigerated for up to 1 week. Place them in an airtight container with sheets of plastic wrap in between the layers.

VARIATIONS:

- Add 1 tablespoon instant espresso powder to the milk for mocha fudge.
- Substitute pure orange extract for the vanilla, and substitute ½ cup chopped candied orange peel and ½ cup dried cranberries for nuts.

✳ ✳

Vassar College, now co-ed but one of the pioneering Seven Sister schools (as the Ivy League for women were called, is the birthplace of fudge. In 1886 Emelyn Hartridge, a Vassar student, reported that this thick confection was being sold in Baltimore for the astronomical sum of 40 cents a pound, so she made thirty pounds of it to raise money for the Vassar Senior Auction. From there its fame spread to other women's colleges such as Mt. Holyoke and Smith, and then into actual cookbooks.

✳ ✳

INDEX

ABOUT CIDER MILL PRESS
BOOK PUBLISHERS

Good ideas ripen with time. From seed to harvest, Cider Mill Press brings fine reading, information, and entertainment together between the covers of its creatively crafted books. Our Cider Mill bears fruit twice a year, publishing a new crop of titles each spring and fall.

Visit us on the Web at
www.cidermillpress.com
or write to us at
12 Port Farm Road
Kennebunkport, Maine 04046